Teacher Certification Exam

Elementary Education
Sample Questions

Written By:

Roberta S. Ramsey, PhD. Professor of
Licensed Professional Counselor

To Order Additional Copies:
Xam, Inc.
99 Central St.
Worcester, MA 01605
Toll Free   1-800-301-4647
Phone: 1-508 363 0633
Email: winwin1111@aol.com
Web   www.xamonline.com
EFax   1-501-325-0185
Fax: 1-508-363-0634

You will find:
- Content Review in prose format
- Bibliography
- Sample Test

XAM, INC.
Building Better Teachers

"And, while there's no reason yet to panic, I think it's only prudent that we make preperations to panic."

MANKOFF

FTCE: Elementary Education Sample Questions
ISBN: 1-58197-064-1

TABLE OF CONTENTS

                                                      Page

HOW TO USE THIS STUDY MANUAL 1

CONTENT AREAS

     Reading and Language Arts 2

     Mathematics 29

     Social Studies 57

     Science 87

     Physical Education and Health 111

     Art, Music, and the Humanities 122

PROFESSIONAL KNOWLEDGE

     Child Growth and Development 135

     Developmental Psychology 144

     Language Development 148

     Special Education Characteristics 153

     Teaching Methods and Strategies 164

     Classroom Management 174

     Special Education Law 178

Reference List **194**

ELEMENTARY SAMPLE QUESTIONS

HOW TO USE THIS STUDY MANUAL

This study manual is written to help teachers prepare for tests for college courses, or for a teacher competency test, also known as the TCT. Questions are presented covering the content of courses that most graduates of elementary education programs complete during teacher training. The correct answer for each of these questions is given, with an explanatory rationale. The questions are grouped into subject content areas and into areas designated as professional knowledge.

Benefits to the user include the following:

1. This practice manual presents study material in a brief, but concise and complete manner. Much essential content is summarized. It is presented in a format that allows for a rationale that explains the correct answer for each sample question given.

2. It helps the test taker to identify those content areas in which the material has been mastered, and those in which more study might be needed.

3. It enables the test taker to have immediate access to facts and information he or she will need to know for a competency test in this field.

4. It provides a quick review for the test taker without his or her having to go back through numerous pages of textbooks and class notes.

5. It saves hours of preparation and study.

GOOD LUCK!

CONTENT AREAS

Reading and Language Arts

1. **It has been suggested that the most effective way to decrease word-by-word reading, and thereby increase more fluid reading, is by helping students to improve their _____ skills.**

   A. Phonetic

   B. Sight vocabulary

   C. Comprehension

   D. Word attack

Answer: B

Rationale (1):   There are a variety of causes for **word-by-word reading**. Word-by-word reading is described as pauses after each word; therefore, producing a **lack of fluency** in reading. Possibilities include an overdependency on use of phonics, lack of comprehension, poor reading habits, and failure to recognize a stock of sight words. Building sight word vocabularies is thought to be the most effective means of remediation.

2. **This term refers to the process of understanding "how" a person thinks and to the process of monitoring one's thinking. It is called**

   A. Cognition.

   B. Metacognition.

   C. Comprehension.

   D. Intellect.

Answer: B

Rationale (2):   **Cognition** is the process of thinking. **Metacognition** is the process of understanding "how" a person thinks. **Metacognition** also includes the process of monitoring one's thoughts.

ELEMENTARY SAMPLE QUESTIONS   2

3. For which of the following purposes for reading would a teacher be most likely to determine whether a student has the necessary background of information and sight vocabulary for reading a particular lesson?

   A. Reinforce

   B. Test

   C. Teach

   D. Administer

Answer: C

Rationale (3): Reading for the purpose of **teaching** requires that the student have the necessary background of meaningful experiences, and be able to recognize the sight vocabulary words in the particular reading passage.

4. Which dimension of reading utilizes clues pertaining to the size, shape, and combinations of letters and sounds, figure-background relationships, relationships of the part to the whole, sequencing, and ordering?

   A. Perceptual

   B. Physiological

   C. Psychological

   D. Linguistic

Answer: A

Rationale (4): The dimensions of reading include social, psychological, physiological, perceptual, linguistic, and intellectual processes. According to Maggart and Zintz (1990), the **perceptual** process utilizes perceptual clues, which include size, shape, combinations of letters and sounds, figure-ground relationships, relationships of the part of the whole, sequencing, and ordering.

5. A descriptor of the linguistic dimension to reading is

    A. Eye-hand coordination

    B. Social acceptance

    C. Memory skills

    D. Understanding of intonation, stress, pauses, and tone sequence

Answer: D

Rationale (5): Maggart and Lintz (1990) describe the **linguistic process** as requiring mastery of phoneme-grapheme relationships, and understanding of intonation, stress, pauses, and tone sequencing. The **linguistic** process also incorporates thought units and understanding of words and ideas as they are presented in context. Social variations are included as language nonstandard usage, figurative language, and slang.

6. _____ is the application of knowledge about consonant and vowel sound clues to the pronunciation of a word.

    A. Synthesis

    B. Phonetic analysis

    C. Configuration

    D. Context cueing

Answer: B

Rationale (6): **Phonetic analysis** is the pronunciation of a word applying knowledge about consonant and vowel clues. Phonic elements include single consonant letters, consonant blends, consonant diagraphs, single vowel letters, vowel diagraphs, and diphthongs.

7. **In spelling, a person writes the letter symbols for the sounds he or she hears. This is called**

   A. Encoding.

   B. Decoding.

Answer: A

Rationale (7): **Decoding** is the process of analyzing phonemes and applying corresponding sounds. Conversely, **encoding** is the process of writing symbols that represent the sounds heard.

8. **_____ is the primary factor now used to determine a youngster's placement by grade level within the school.**

   A. Learning age

   B. Age expectancy

   C. Chronological age

   D. Mental age

Answer: C

Rationale (8): American education had its origins in one-room schoolhouses with heterogeneous age groupings. In the late 1800s, Horace Mann established the grade level system which grouped students by **chronological ages**. This system for grouping by relatively homogenous ages is still utilized today.

9. The range of student differences in a given classroom will _____ through the year and from year-to-year as the class progresses through school.

   A. Increase

   B. Decrease

Answer: A

Rationale (9): The reading level of a sample class has been defined as that level at which the "middle child" reads. On a standardized test, this measure is the level above which and below which half the students in a class read. The range within a class will **increase** each year with good teaching, because each child is able to reach his or her own capacity.

10. Which of the following words is one of the twelve most frequently used words that appear in children's reading books?

   A. There

   B. This

   C. The

   D. An

Answer: C

Rationale (10): The twelve **most frequently used words** identified by McNally and Murray (1968) are: a, and, he, I, in, is, it, of, that, the, to, and was. These words account for about 25 percent of the running words in their print sample.

11. **The Wide Range Achievement Test - Revised (WRAT-R) is a standardized screening test that measures performance in spelling, math computation, and the reading skill of**

   A. Word recognition

   B. Reading comprehension

   C. Word attack

   D. Word configuration

Answer: A

Rationale (11): The WRAT-R is a standardized test that measures word recognition, spelling, and arithmetic computation. This is a screening test because it tests **word recognition** skills solely. It does not test comprehension, word attack, and other reading skills which are also measured when administering a diagnostic test.

12. **The Dolch Basic Sight Words consist of a relatively short list of words that children should be able to**

   A. Sound out

   B. Know the meaning of

   C. Recognize at sight

   D. Use in a sentence

Answer: C

Rationale (12): The Dolch Basic Sight Words consists of a list of 220 words. These are the most common words that appear in reading materials. In fact, this list of "service" words make up over half of all the running words that children read in textbook series.

13. Which type of reading test is one in which the teacher reads one word in each row of four words and asks the child to find and circle it?

   A. Recall

   B. Recognition

Answer: B

Rationale (13); There are two methods for testing knowledge of basic sight vocabulary. In a **recognition** test, the teacher reads one word in each row of four words and asks the student to locate and circle or point to it. A recall test requires the student to say each word from recall or memory. The teacher has a better measure of the sight words a child knows when the child is asked to pronounce every word in each row while progressing down the page.

14. The _____ level of reading is the highest level at which a child can read fluently and with personal satisfaction without help.

   A. Independent

   B. Instructional

   C. Frustration

Answer: A

15. When administering an informal reading inventory (IRI), the _____ level is the highest level at which a child makes no more than five incorrect miscues in reading one hundred running words with at least 75 percent comprehension of the ideas in the reading passage.

   A. Independent

   B. Instructional

   C. Frustration

   D. Capacity

Answer: B

16. The _____ level measures the level at which readers would function if they were able to use all of their innate abilities (e.g., listening, understanding) in place of reading.

   A. Independent

   B. Instructional

   C. Frustration

   D. Capacity

Answer: D

Rationale (14-16): The IRI (informal reading inventory) is an individual test which the student reads both silently and orally. The inventory contains increasingly difficult material at each level.

   The **independent level** is the highest level at which he or she can read fluently and with personal pleasure without assistance. Only one miscue in a reading passage of one hundred words is made, and 90 percent comprehension is obtained when measured.

   The **instructional level** is the level at which the student is taught. At this level the child makes no more than five miscues that he or she is unable to correct in one hundred running words with at least 75 percent correct responses to comprehension questions.

   The **frustration level** is the lowest level of reading for the individual. More than ten miscues are made in one hundred running words and at least 50 percent incorrect responses are made to comprehension questions.

   The **capacity level** for reading is the highest level at which the student can understand the ideas and information presented in the reading material when it is read aloud by the teacher or by classmates for the individual. The same comprehension standard set for the instructional level, that of 75 percent, is also used for establishing a student's level of capacity.

17. **Jerome recently began preschool. He is having difficulty with sound-symbol relationships and auditory discrimination of sounds. When Jerome's mother visited the school, it was discovered that Spanish is the primary language spoken in the home. Jerome's difficulty with phonemes is probably due to which variable?**

   A. Cultural deprivation

   B. Cognitive thinking

   C. Language exposure

   D. Family motivation

Answer: C

Rationale (17): Students exposed to more than one language at home during preschool years may experience phonemic difficulties with sound-symbol relationships, as well as discrimination between the phonemic pronunciations and graphic symbols of the various languages.

18. **David's fifth grade teacher discovered by informal testing that David could recognize very few basic vocabulary words. His teacher therefore took a large tablet of chart paper and wrote a few sentences each day that David dictated to her about his life on a farm. David read, copied, and reread these sentences like a story book. This language experience approach was beneficial to David primarily because**

   A. He learned left-to-right eye movement

   B. He learned to read words from his own speaking vocabulary

   C. His teacher stressed reading comprehension

   D. He practiced writing sentences from a chart

Answer: B

Rationale (18): In the **language experience approach**, the teacher writes the verbal statements made by students onto a lined chart. This approach is successful with many students because the student's thoughts are recorded on the charts as a short story of one or two paragraphs in length. The sentences in this short story make up reading selection, and include vocabulary words from the student's own speaking vocabulary.

ELEMENTARY SAMPLE QUESTIONS

19. **Mrs. William is certain that five-year-old Terry will not be ready to begin work in a pre-primer reading book because of his difficulty with left-right orientation. Which of the reading readiness activities listed below would most likely help Terry to develop this skill?**

    A. Have him practice visually tracking a moving object around the classroom

    B. Play "Simon Says" with him

    C. Have Terry repeat the directions to the teacher

    D. Use arrow cues or color coding on worksheets to prompt directionality

Answer: D

Rationale (19): **Left-right orientation** is an essential pre-reading skill. The child must learn to begin at the correct place and proceed using left-to-right progression. It is important for the teacher to use instructional activities and cues that strengthen directionality, such as color coding and placement of arrows.

20. **Basic sight words refer to high frequency words that appear often in print and are included in basic word lists. Which is the best example of a basic word list?**

    A. Dolch Word List

    B. Survival words

    C. A spelling list of words

    D. Webster's Dictionary

Answer: A

Rationale (20): The Dolch Word List is comprised of words that are used most frequently in basal reading materials. The words are taken from each graded reading level and total 220.

21. **Teachers rather than teaching devices have the most control over the presentation of vocabulary words when using which of the following modes of presentation?**

    A. Language Master

    B. Computer software

    C. Flash cards

    D. Speed reading machines

Answer: C

Rationale (21): Teachers have the most control over the use of **flash cards** when presenting vocabulary words to students. Words can be selected at the time of presentation from survival lists of words, basal reading textbooks, and prevalent word lists. Flash cards can be included, omitted, repeated, highlighted, incorporated into small group games, and even given to the students to take home for drill and practice. Teaching devices are less flexible and more restrictive in use.

22. **When the teacher supplies students with a list of contractions and asks them to write the two words for each contraction on the list that mean the same, she is teaching them specific skills in**

    A. Configuration clues

    B. Structural analysis

    C. Decoding

    D. Phonetic analysis

Answer: B

Rationale (22): In **structural analysis**, structural cues are analyzed to decode derived and inflected words. The term structural analysis refers to larger parts of words that bear meaning such as root words, suffixes, prefixes, word endings, apostrophe plus "s" to show possession, contractions, and compound words.

23. Mrs. Green leaves spaces in sentences within given reading passages. She is attempting to help students become more proficient in the use of

A. Sight vocabulary

B. Comprehension strategies

C. Synonyms

D. Context clues

Answer: D

Rationale (23): The clues or hints a student receives from a word by the way it is used in the context of a sentence is called **context cueing**. Another way of providing context cueing is to use pictures or illustrations that correspond with the written words or passages.

24. Advance organizers are used primarily to

A. Help students focus on main ideas or concepts within the chapter before they begin reading

B. Help students recall main ideas or concepts within a selected reading after it is read

C. Quiz students, section-by-section, about what they are reading

D. Assist students in summarizing what they have read

Answer: A

Rationale (24): There are several ways in which students can be alerted to or asked questions about important content they are about to read. **Advance organizers** provide a list of main ideas or concepts about which the student is preparing to read. Students are more likely to focus upon the content that explains these ideas.

25. Which of the following questions would be appropriate to ask a student whose inferential comprehension was being assessed?

    A. Where did Snow White go to hide from the wicked queen?

    B. How many years did Rapunzel spend in the tower?

    C. Why do you think Goldilocks found Baby Bear's things to be just right?

    D. What was Little Red Riding Hood taking to her grandmother?

Answer: C

Rationale (25): Most educators recognize that comprehension covers a broad range of lower-to-higher level thinking skills. **Inferential** comprehension is one of the levels of comprehension skills. It involves an understanding of the deeper meanings that are not literally stated in a phrase, sentence, or passage. In the questions listed in this example, the reader must infer reasons that Goldilocks found Baby Bear's things to be just right since this is not specifically stated in the story.

26. Mrs. Smith observed her daughter, Jackie, to be crying while she was reading the novel, A Lady, A Champion. When Mrs. Smith asked Jane what was wrong, Jane replied, "It makes me feel sad that Angela's father died. He was just a poor, older man whose life was changed when he became disabled during the war. If I became a famous swimmer like her, I would want my dad to around to see it!" Angela's response showed that she was identifying and making an emotional response to the characters in the story. To which higher-order thinking level was Jane's response?

    A. Literal

    B. Inferential

    C. Evaluative

    D. Appreciative

Answer: D

Rationale (26): The **appreciation** level of comprehension skills deals with the psychological and aesthetic impact of the selection on the reader. This occurs when the reader 1) makes an emotional response to the content, 2) identifies with characters or incidents, 3) reacts to the author's use of language, or it occurs 4) through imagery.

27. **Mrs. Allen has constructed an informal reading inventory (IRI) to assist her in placing her students in appropriate basal readers for reading instruction. When constructing the word recognition test for one of a series of the basal readers, the teacher might count the total number of words in the glossary. If her total count is 360 words, and she wants a total of 20 words in her teacher-made IRI, then she will include every _____ word, regardless of its simplicity or complexity.**

    A. 18th

    B. 20th

    C. 25th

    D. 30th

Answer: A

Rationale (27): If Mrs. Allen wants to develop a vocabulary list containing 20 words for her teacher-made informal reading inventory (IRI), then she will divide the total words in the basal reading book's glossary, 360 words, by the length of the proposed list, 20 words, and include every 18th word.

28. **One of the passages in the informal reading inventory developed by Mrs. Allen is a story about a boy whose family buys a monkey from the pet store. The story describes both the pleasures and the problems incurred by this family's choice of pet. If the reader is later asked to elaborate upon whether he or she would like for his family to get a monkey as a pet, this question would be characteristic of what type of thinking skill?**

    A. Literal recall

    B. Reorganization

    C. Inferential

    D. Evaluation

Answer: D

Rationale (28): Comprehension at the **evaluation** level requires the reader to make a judgment by comparing ideas presented in the selection with external criteria provided by the teacher, or by some other external source, or with internal criteria provided by the student him or herself.

ELEMENTARY SAMPLE QUESTIONS

29. **Mrs. Allen recorded four errors in word recognition and two in comprehension while using the IRI. If the story being read was on a third grade level with 100 running words in the content, and ten questions were asked to determine comprehension, it can be said that this student's performance shows this level reader to be on his _____ level.**

   A. Independent

   B. Instructional

   C. Frustration

   D. Recreational

Answer: B

Rationale (29): An IRI is used to identify a student's level of reading at the **independent**, **instructional**, and **frustration levels**. Instruction should occur at the level where no more than five errors are recorded during a reading sample of 100 words, and comprehension questions are answered correctly at 75 percent or above. At the student's independent reading level, he or she would miss only one word in a one-hundred word passage and answer 90 percent of the questions correct. Frustration is reached when the student makes ten errors or more in a one-hundred word passage and answers 50 percent or less of the comprehension questions asked.

30. **The word "happy" is an example of a**

   A. Free morpheme

   B. Bound morpheme

Answer: A

Rationale (30): **Morphemes** are the smallest meaning-bearing units in our language system. Morphemes that can stand alone in meaning, like "happy," are called **free morphemes**. On the other hand, if we added the "un" morpheme to the word happy, the "un" could not stand alone and would be called a **bound** morpheme.

31. **"The deletion, organization, and interpretation of information" describes which cognitive process?**

   A. Reflection

   B. Insight

   C. Perception

   D. Memory

Answer: C

Rationale (31): **Perception** is the deletion, organization, and interpretation of information. The evaluation of the quality of ideas and solutions is called **reflection**, and the recognition of new relationships between two or more segments of knowledge is known as **insight**. **Memory** is the storage and retrieval of received information.

32. **Different meanings of words can be categorized through the webbing process. The word "swaggered" would best illustrate which of the categories that define the word "went?"**

   A. Happy

   B. Tired

   C. Proud

   E. Frightened

Answer: C

Rationale (32): Words that can be used in place of "went" include categories depicting "proud, slow, happy, tired, and frightened" meanings. A "proud" meaning would include words like "swaggered, strutted, pranced, and promenaded."

33. **The lowercase letter that is least similar when written in manuscript and cursive alphabet is**

    A. a

    B. d

    C. j

    D. u

Answer: C

Rationale (33): Some lowercase letters that are similar in manuscript and cursive alphabets are: a, d, g, h, I, l, m, n, o, p, q, t, u, and y. Similar capital letters are: B, C, K, L, O, P, R, and U.

34. **When checking the words on Susie's spelling paper, her teacher noticed that Susie spelled the word "stand" as "stan." Her spelling error is which of the following?**

    A. A silent letter is omitted

    B. A sounded letter is omitted

    C. A single letter is added

    D. There is a non-phonetic substitution for a vowel

Answer: B

Rationale (34): Spache's Spelling Errors Test provides a list of "types of errors" often reflected in children's spelling. These include:
1) A sounded letter is omitted (e.g., stand - stan).
2) A single letter is added (e.g., mark - marck).
3) There is a nonphonetic substitution for a vowel (e.g., ground - grade).
4) There is a phonetic substitution for a vowel (e.g., team - teme).

35. Susie's teacher also saw that Susie spelled the word "angel" as "angle." Which of the spelling errors identified by Spache did she make?

    A. A double letter is omitted

    B. Letters are transposed or reversed

    C. There is a phonetic substitution for the syllable

    D. A silent letter is omitted

Answer: B

Rationale (35): According to Spache, other types of errors reflected in children's spelling are:
1) Letters are transposed or reversed (e.g., angel - angle).
2) A double letter is omitted (e.g., supper - super).
3) There is a phonetic substitution for the syllable (e.g., enjoys - enjoies).

36. Horne (1963) recommended teaching spelling rules that apply to a large number of words and have few exceptions. Mrs. Brown taught this generalization to her 4th grade students: If a word ends with a consonant plus "y," change the "y" to "I" before adding suffixes except those beginning with "i." Do not change the "y" to "I" when adding suffixes to words ending in a vowel plus "y." Which of the following examples does NOT follow this generalization?

    A. Carrying

    B. Babies

    C. Enjoying

    D. Buoys

Answer: C

Rationale (36): The following illustrate the generalization given.
1) The man was enjo_____ the game. (ying)
2) The boy was carry _____ his lunch. (ing)
3) The bab_____ looked cute. (ies)
4) The buoy _____ were bobbing in the waves. (s)

ELEMENTARY SAMPLE QUESTIONS   19

37. The "present tense" is stated in which sentence?

    A. Sam plays basketball today.

    B. Sam played basketball yesterday.

    C. Sam will play basketball tomorrow.

Answer: A

Rationale (37): The tense of a verb tells when the action or the state of being occurs--in the **present**, in the **past**, or in the **future**. The sentences given illustrate present, past, and future, in that order.

38. The sentence that states the thought in "past perfect tense" is

    A. Jim has written a story.

    B. Jim had written a story.

    C. Jim will have written a story.

Answer: B

Rationale (38): A perfect tense is one in which an action or a state of being has been completed--in the **present**, in the **past**, or in the **future**. The sentences listed demonstrate these, in the order stated.

39. Which is stated correctly?

    A. John spoke to you and I.

    B. He said for you and I to go home.

    C. You and me can go now.

    D. It is okay for you and me to go there.

Answer: D

Rationale (39): "You," "I," and "me" are pronouns. "I" is a subjective personal pronoun; whereas, "me" is a objective personal pronoun. "You" can be both. In example "d," the words you and me form the subject of a clause.

40. Which adverb has a superlative ending?

    A. Soon

    B. Sooner

    C. Soonest

Answer: C

Rationale (40): Adverbs can describe verbs, other adverbs, and adjectives. A few adverbs take the comparative "er" and superlative "est" ending, like soon, sooner, and soonest.

41. **"I'll go if she will." In this sentence, the word "if" is which part of speech?**

    A. Conjunction

    B. Preposition

    C. Pronoun

    D. Interjection

Answer: A

Rationale (41): **Conjunctions** connect words, groups of words, or whole sentences. The most commonly used conjunctions are: "and, or, but."

42. **"Write the words on the chalkboard." Sentences like this that make a request or a command are _____ sentences.**

    A. Declarative

    B. Interrogative

    C. Exclamatory

    D. Imperative

Answer: D

Rationale (42): An **imperative** sentence states a command or makes a request. **Declarative** sentences make statements, **interrogative** sentences ask questions, and **exclamatory** sentences express strong feelings or sudden emotions.

43. What is the "predicate" of this sentence? "He is a good student."

    A. He

    B. good student

    C. is

    D. is a good student

Answer: D

Rationale (43): The **predicate** always contains a verb and is the word or group of words that tells what is being said about the subject.

44. "If you go, I'll go." A comma is used in this sentence because

    A. It is taking the place of "and" or "or" in a series of three or more words

    B. The dependent clause is first in this complex sentence containing two clauses

    C. It is being used to separate a series of adjectives that modify the same noun or pronoun

    D. A parenthetical expression is present

Answer: B

Rationale (44): Of the above reasons for using a comma in a sentence, a comma is used in this sentence because the dependent clause is first in this complex sentence containing two clauses.

45. The _____ level measures the level at which readers would function if they were able to use all of their innate abilities (e.g., listening, understanding) in place of reading.

    A. Independent

    B. Instructional

    C. Frustration

    D. Capacity

Answer: D

Rationale (45): The **capacity level** measures the level at which readers would function if they were able to use all of their innate abilities like listening and understanding in place of reading.

46. A syllable is a word or part of a word that has only one vowel _____.

    A. Letter

    B. Sound

    C. Symbol

    D. Marking

Answer: B

Rationale (46): A syllable is a word, or part of a word, that has only one vowel sound. A one-syllable word may have two vowels, but only one vowel is sounded. A polysyllabic word has as many syllables as it has separate vowel sounds.

47. Syllables are classified as open or closed. "Closed" syllables are those that end with a

    A. Vowel sound

    B. Consonant sound

    C. Suffix

    D. Comparative ending

Answer: B

Rationale (47): Closed syllables end with a consonant sound (e.g., sun set). Open syllables end with a vowel sound (e.g., famous).

48. Which of the two consonant combinations listed is an example of a consonant diagraph?

    A. "Ch" in chicken

    B. "Cl" in clean

    C. "Fl" in flag

    D. "Ed" in jumped

Answer: a

Rationale (48): A consonant diagraph is a combination of two letters that result in a single speech sound. This sound is a "new" sound, unlike the sounds made by the individual consonants. Consonant diagraphs include: "th" in that and thicket; "sh" in ship, "ch" in chicken, choral and chute; "ph;" "gh;" "ng;" and "nk."

49. The letter "g" has two sounds. The hard sound of "g" is heard in the word

 A. George

 B. Great

 C. Go

 D. Large

Answer: C

Rationale (49): The letter "g" represents two sounds: hard and soft. The **hard** sound of "g" is heard in the word "game." The **soft** sound is heard as "j" as in the word "gentle."

50. An example of a function or structure word that serves as a noun marker is

 A. Am

 B. How

 C. The

 D. Who

Answer: C

Rationale (50): Words that have no referents are called function or structure words. It is estimated that these function words, though no more than 300 in everyday English, comprise almost half of the words in early reading content.

   These kinds of words are called markers for the types of structured elements they precede: noun, verb, phrase, clause, and question markers. Noun markers include "a," "the," "some," and "three."

51. **"Cause and effect" thinking has a relationship with which type of organization skill?**

    A. Summarizing

    B. Underlining

    C. Outlining

    D. Sequencing

Answer: D

Rationale (51): Sequencing is related to outlining, but it has broader implications. Students are taught to recall sequential happenings in their own lives. This helps them to understand the sequences in the lives of others, and in the sequential progressions of places, events, and so on.

52. **Everyone seemed to understand what Mary meant when she said, "I was stuck with the job!" Mary was describing how she felt when she was assigned a task none of her classmates wanted. Her utterance is an example of a (an)**

    A. Idiom

    B. Slang expression

    C. Metaphor

    D. Analogy

Answer: A

Rationale (52): Semantic differences can be found in common **idionetic expressions**, multiple meanings of common words, simple analogies, and word opposites. Idioms carry meaning other than the literal one. Examples include: "He's a big wheel!" "His reply let the cat out of the bag." "Stop horsing around." "She's feeling blue."

53. A tachistoscope is a teaching aid that enables a student to

A. See a column of words at one time

B. View a single word in a list of words

C. Study the entire page of words at one time

Answer: B

Rationale (53): Tachistoscopes are essentially "window boxes" that enable a teacher to present isolated words to students in order to practice recognition of vocabulary words. This device displays words one at a time through an open space.

54. Mark and his teacher, Mrs. Green, both read aloud together. When Mrs. Green determines that Mark is doing fine, she lowers her voice so that Mark carries the responsibility. However, whenever Mark does not know a word, Mrs. Green continues reading. The name for this method for teaching reading is

A. Choral reading

B. Cloze procedure

C. Shadow reading (or impress method)

D. Sustained silent reading

Answer: C

Rationale (54): The neurological impress method increases reading skills by having the child and the teacher read passages simultaneously. "Shadow reading" is a type of **impress method** described by Frostig as the oral reading of a particular passage by the teacher and student simultaneously. When the child is reading successfully, the teacher lowers his or her voice so that the student assumes the primary reading task. Then when the youngster does not recognize a word, the teacher goes on reading until the child can again read successfully.

Mathematics

1. **Marcia, a preschooler, was asked to sort toys familiar to her. When given a large car, she was able to tell why it did not belong with a group of matchbox cars. By doing so, Marcia was demonstrating the ability to classify objects by**

   A. Function

   B. Color

   C. Size

   D. Shape

Answer: C

2. **John was given a closed container into which he could insert geometric shapes in the lid. By being able to one-by-one place squares, triangles, and rectangles into the holes of those shapes, John successfully showed the ability to classify by**

   A. Function

   B. Color

   C. Size

   D. Shape

Answer: D

Rationales (1 & 2): The development of arithmetic abilities is based upon the child's ability to classify. **Classification** refers to "the ability to group objects according to some distinguishing characteristic" (Ramsey, 1995, p. 201). The child must become able to discriminate between objects on the basis of some relevant aspect of function, such as size, shape, color, and form, as well as by several criteria at the same time.

3. **Jane was able to place a series of rings of graduated sizes on a cone. By doing so she was able to demonstrate the ability to perform which type of seriation task?**

   A. Linear

   B. Unit

   C. Temporal

   D. One-to-one correspondence

   E. Spatial relations

Answer: A

Rationale (3): Our entire number system in mathematics depends upon the ability to seriate. **Seriation**, or ordering, is demonstrated by a young child when he or she successfully places a series of rings of graduated sizes on a cone, or places graduated sizes of cups into a nesting arrangement. More complex seriation tasks involve "lining up objects of graduated height or diameter in ascending order" (Ramsey, 1995, p. 202). The child eventually is able to seriate on the basis of numbers in a series of sets.

4. **By being able to state why a lump of clay is the same whether it is rolled into a ball or into a string, a youngster is demonstrating the concept of**

   A. Classification

   B. Seriation

   C. Conservation

Answer: C

Rationale (4): The concept of **conservation** refers to the fact that "the number of units within an object (or set) remains the same regardless of changes made in the shape of the unit or the arrangement of the set" (Ramsey, 1995, p. 202). Conservation is related closely to reversibility. It is necessary to understand reversibility in order to understand the relationship between addition and subtraction.

5. **Ann's mother told her that she could have the "third" piece of birthday cake as slices were given to friends. By being able to understand when she was to receive her piece of cake, Ann was showing skill in use of _____ numbers.**

   A. Ordinal

   B. Cardinal

   C. Even

   D. Odd

Answer: A

Rationale (5): **Ordinal** numbers specify the relative position or order of an object within a set in relation to the other objects (e.g., first, second, last, and so on). **Cardinal** numbers identify the number of objects referred to with a group. In other words, these numbers answer the question of "How many?"

6. **Which of the following activities needs to come first when helping a youngster to develop a conceptual understanding of adding 6 and 3?**

   A. Using numerals to write the problem 6 + 3

   B. Having the child arrange blocks in groups of 6 and 3

   C. Showing pictures of objects in groups of 6 and 3

   D. Introducing families to demonstrate 6 + 3 = 9, 3 + 6 = 9, 9 - 6 + 3, 9 - 3 = 6

Answer: B

Rationale (6): A child must be able to perform certain prerequisite tasks before beginning formal instruction in mathematics. Being able to "match, sort, compare, and arrange objects" precedes being able to perform the other tasks listed.

7. **Students in Miss Trip's fourth grade were having a difficult time memorizing assigned multiplication facts. Miss Trip realized she was going to have to back up and provide prerequisite learning experiences. Which is the most "basic" of the experiences she   might plan for her math class?**

  A. Use concrete manipulatives to make groups of equal size

  B. Present pictorial representations of groupings with sets of equal-size

  C. Drill and practice with flash cards

  D. Write number facts ten times each

Answer: A

Rationale (7): In order to achieve meaningful understanding, it is important that instruction in mathematics begin at the concrete, manipulative level. Instruction should then progress to pictorial representations, and finally, to the abstract, symbolic level.

8. Miss Smith, the student teacher in Mrs. Walker's third grade classroom, went through a carefully planned introduction to basic multiplication procedures before beginning a unit. Miss Smith had the students look at the groupings with sets of equal-size shown in their text. She then drew these same sets on the chalkboard. Finally, Miss Smith assigned several of the multiplication problems to be done on worksheets. As she checked the students' work, Miss Smith found many did not understand the basic procedure of multiplying. Mrs. Walker explained to Miss Smith that the majority of her introduction was on a (n) _____ level, and needed to have been presented on a(n) _____ level to assure better understanding by all students.

   A. Concrete, abstract

   B. Pictorial, concrete

   C. Abstract, pictorial

   D. Abstract, concrete

Answer: B

Rationale (8): Too often, the pictorial representations in textbooks are used in instruction as the basic level for understanding; therefore, omitting the hands-on concrete, manipulative level, which is necessary for meaningful understanding in later conceptual knowledge at the abstract, symbolic level. That is what Miss Smith did in her instruction in the example given.

9. **Multiplication is essentially**

   A. The combining of equal-size sets

   B. Repeated addition

   C. The reversible concept associated with division

   D. All of the above

Answer: D

Rationale (9): Multiplication is initially taught as repeated addition. It includes the "combining" of two or more equal-size sets to form a new set. Division is the inverse operation of multiplication in that the total is "separated" into groups of equal-size sets.

ELEMENTARY SAMPLE QUESTIONS   33

10. In this subtraction problem, which number is the minuend?

$$\begin{array}{r} 1{,}263 \\ -465 \\ \hline 798 \end{array}$$

A. 1,263

B. 465

C. 798

Answer: A

Rationale (10): The total or top number in a subtraction problem is called the **minuend**. The amount that is taken away or the bottom number is called the **subtrahend**. The difference between the two numbers is called the **remainder**.

11. The word "root" in mathematics means

A. The base of a tree which provides nutrients and stability

B. The number which when multiplied by itself produces the square or other product

C. The attachment portions of a tooth

D. The actions of a pig in a barnyard

Answer: B

Rationale (11): Students need to be taught appropriate mathematical terminology. Many words have a different meaning when used in a mathematical context than when used in everyday life. Examples of such words include "root," "order," "base," "power," and "set."

12. **When checking John's homework, Mr. Taylor discovered that John had forgotten to borrow from the tens place when subtracting the minuend from the subtrahend in several of the assigned problems. In fact, of the twelve problems, John had made this error four times. Mr. Taylor concluded that John had, in essence, made "one" processing error in his regrouping procedures for borrowing from two digit numbers in subtraction. Mr. Taylor deduced this difficulty by using which strategy?**

   A. Work out difficult words

   B. Determine the overall picture

   C. Discover semantic relationships among words, phrases, and clauses

   D. None of the above

Answer: B

Rationale (13): Knowing how to utilize sequential problem-solving processes in solving verbal mathematical problems is essential. The student first reads the math problem to identify the overall picture or pattern stated. During the second reading, difficult words or concepts are worked out. Finally, the problem is read again to determine semantic and logical relationships among words, phrases, and clauses. The planning of which processes need to be used to obtain a mathematical solution is done during this last reading as well.

14. **In mathematical language, which is considered to be an "exclusionary" rather than an inclusionary term?**

   A. Left

   B. Some

   C. All

   D. More

Answer: A

Rationale (14): In mathematical language, inclusionary and exclusionary words carry specific meanings. Examples of **inclusionary** words are "all," "some," "more," and "few." Some examples of **exclusionary** words are "except," "left," and "remainder."

15. A skill that is not a part of problem-solving is

   A. Analyzing situations

   B. Hypothesizing results

   C. Rendering value judgments

   D. Using trial and error during inquiry

Answer: C

Rationale (15): Problem-solving skills include posing questions; analyzing situations; hypothesizing, translating, and illustrating results; drawing diagrams; and using trial and error.

16. Mrs. Gray told her students that over 3,000 persons had assembled at the town square for a march. To which of these concepts was Mrs. Gray making reference?

   A. Area

   B. Mass

   C. Perimeter

   D. Volume

Answer: D

Rationale (16): A group of people gathered together represents a **mass**; that is, a large quantity, amount, or number. The **area** is the surface included within a set of lines, specifically, the number of unit squares equal in measure to the surface. The **perimeter** represents the outer limits of an area, and **volume** is space occupied as measured in cubic units (as inches, quarts, or pecks).

17. Which does not define or describe the term ratio?

A. The term proportion is synonymous

B. The indicated quotient of two mathematical expressions.

C. The relationship in quantity, amount, or size between two or more things.

D. It is a share determined by supply.

Answer: D

Rationale (17): The answer "d" defines the term ration. All of the other answers, "a," "b," and "c," either define or describe what is meant by **ratio**.

18. Which is a prime number?

A. 1

B. 17

C. 25

D. 18

Answer: B

Rationale (18): A **prime number** is a positive integer that is greater than one and has no factor or divisors except itself and one.

19. **What is the next number in this sequence? 9, 13, ___, 24, 31.**

    A. 17

    B. 18

    C. 19

    D. 20

Answer: B

Rationale (19): Beginning with a difference of 4, each number given increases by 1 more. Since the unknown number is next in sequence, the differential interval is "5" or "1 more than 4."

20. **Fred's teacher used error analysis to find what type of mistake Fred was making when attempting to regroup numbers in addition problems. What is the error the teacher would conclude is causing Fred to miss the most math problems?**

167	323	981	1,045	3,417
+37	+93	+41	+ 976	+ 894
194	316	922	1,911	3,201

    A. Fred adds from left to right

    B. Fred does not carry over the sums greater than 9 into the next column

    C. Fred does not keep the columns in vertical order

    D. Fred miscalculates basic sums

Answer: B

Rationale (20): In each problem, Fred has calculated the sums correctly, has kept the columns vertically aligned, and has added from right to left. His error is failing to carry over the extra digit from sums greater than 9 into the next column.

21. **Bobby stopped to purchase a treat on the way home. When he went to pay the sales clerk, Bobby found he was short a dime. His friend Lee, who was in line behind him, loaned Bobby the dime. How much did the treat cost Bobby? Evaluation of this problem indicates that the information given is**

  A. Adequate

  B. Extraneous

  C. Insufficient

  D. Remote

Answer: C

Rationale (21): **Insufficient** information is given to solve this math reasoning problem.

22-24. **An airline has three flights each day from Columbus, Georgia to Detroit, Michigan. The early flight can carry 396 passengers on a jumbo jet. The mid-day and late flights can each carry 137 people on regular jets. Apply this information to solve the next three problems.**

  22. **How many passengers can be flown to Detroit on these flights?**

    A. 533

    B. 670

    C. 274

    D. 660

Answer: B

22. **How many more passengers can travel on the early flight in one week than on both of the regular flights combined?**

    A. 854

    B. 1,813

    C. 122

    D. 670

Answer: A

23. **If jumbo jets were not available for the morning flight, how many regular jet flights would it take to haul the same number of passengers as the jumbo jet in one week?**

    A. No change

    B. 3 flights per morning, on the smaller planes

    C. 5 flights per morning, on the smaller planes

    D. 3 flights per morning, on the smaller planes

Answer: B

Rationales (22-24): By adding 396 + 137(2), we get 670, the total number of passengers per day. By subtracting (2 X 137) from 396, we see that 122 less passengers per day can ride on both smaller jets. We find that 122 X 7 yields 854 more passengers per week. If the jumbo jets were not available for the morning flight, we would need to haul 396 more people on the smaller flights. Divide this number by 137 and we see that two full flights plus a partially full plane with 122 remaining passengers are required, or three flights.

25. What is the value of "6" in "3462?"

 A. 600

 B. 60

 C. 6000

 D. 6

Answer: B

Rationale (25): The number "6" is located in the tens place when analyzing place value amounts. Therefore, the value is "60."

26. Wednesday's attendance at the Braves baseball game was 47,679. On Friday, 72,433 attended their game. An estimated rounding off to the nearest thousand of the total attendance for both days is

 A. 120,112

 B. 130,000

 C. 119,000

 D. 120,000

Answer: D

Rationale (26): Answer "a" is the actual sum, not the rounded off sum. Answer "b" has raised the thousands column up on both days, which is wrong for Friday. Answer "c" has rounded the thousands columns downward for both days, which is wrong for Wednesday. Answer "d" combines 48,000 and 72,000, which is correct.

27. **Four students were given a large circle and asked to measure the diameter. Tim thought they should measure a line segment joining any two points on a circle. Mary suggested that they measure a segment from any point on a circle to its center. Jane said they needed to measure two points around the perimeter of the circle. Larry stated that they needed to measure the line segment passing through the center of the circle and joining two points of a circle. Which student was correct?**

    A. Tim

    B. Mary

    C. Jane

    D. Larry

Answer: D

Rationale (27): The **diameter** is the length of a straight line through the center of a circle; thus, Larry had the correct solution.

28. **List the fractions in order from least to greatest in value. 1/3, 2/8, 5/10, 7/8.**

    A. 1/3, 2/8, 7/8, 5/10

    B. 2/8, 1/3, 5/10, 7/8

    C. 2/8, 7/8, 1/3, 5/10

    D. 5/10, 1/3, 2/8, 7/8

Answer: B

Rationale (28): First one might reduce the fractions shown to their greatest common factor. Thus, 2/8 would reduce to 1/4 and 5/10 would reduce to 1/2. Now the fractions can be seen visually imaged and the obvious sequence from least to greatest in value is 2/8, 1/3, 5/10, and 7/8.

29. Which number is the numerator in the following fraction? 3/4

A. 3

B. 7

C. 4

D. 1

Answer: A

Rationale (29): The **numerator** is the term in a fraction which indicates the number of fractional units present. In a common fraction like "3/4," the numerator is written above the line.

30. What is the common denominator for the following fractions?
3/4, 2/8, 1/2, 5/16

A. 4

B. 8

C. 2

D. 16

Answer: D

Rationale (30): In simple fractions, the **denominator** is the part of the fraction below the line that states into how many equal parts the unit is supposed to be divided. The **common denominator** is the number into which all denominators of the fractions listed can be divided. The answer is 16.

31. Solve the following. What is "n?" $\dfrac{n}{3} = \dfrac{25}{15}$

    A. 5

    B. 3

    C. 10

    D. 12

Answer: A

Rationale (31): This equation lends itself to cross multiplication. We can say that $15n = 75$, divide both sides by 15, and determine that $n = 5$.

32. Of the 80 boats at Captain Bobby's Boat Lot, 40 percent are used rather than new. Of these, 25, percent are more than three years old. How many boats at Captain Bobby's are new or used but less than three years old?

    A. 32

    B. 72

    C. 8

    D. 56

Answer: B

Rationale (32): We multiply 40% X 80 and find that 32 boats are used. Of these, 25% or (1/4) are older than three years, which is 8 boats. So, 80 - 8 gives the total of boats that are either new or used but less than three years old.

33. Twenty-five hundredths is also written

    A. .25

    B. 2.5

    C. .025

    D. .0025

Answer: A

Rationale (33): The 25 is written in the hundredths place when written as a decimal ".25."

34. Write this decimal as a fraction: 8.25 .

    A. 8/250

    B. 8/25

    C. 8 25/100

    D. 825/100

Answer: C

Rationale (34): Eight and twenty-five one hundredths as a fraction is written "8 25/100."

35. What is the following product? 10^5 X .36 = _____

    A. 3,600

    B. 360

    C. 360,000

    D. 36,000

Answer: D

Rationale (35): Ten to the fifth power is 100,000. This amount times .36 yields 36,000.

36-39. Convert each of the following:

36. 56 months to years and months

    A. 4 years 4 months

    B. 4 years 8 months

    C. 2 years 11 months

    D. 2 years 6 months

Answer: B

37. 63 hours to days and hours

    A. 4 days 4 hours

    B. 4 days 8 hours

    C. 2 days 15 hours

    D. 2 days 6 hours

Answer: C

38. Convert 52 inches to feet and inches

    A. 4 feet 4 inches

    B. 4 feet 8 inches

    C. 2 feet 11 inches

    D. 3 feet 10 inches

Answer: A

39. **Convert 78 inches to yards and inches**

    A. 4 yards 4 inches

    B. 4 yards 8 inches

    C. 2 yards 15 inches

    D. 2 yards 6 inches

Answer: D

Rationales (36-39): In each case, we convert the largest whole number of the larger units (years, days, feet, and yards), then express what is left over in the smaller units. A common error is to work in units of ten, which British measures do not do.

40-41. Perform each of the following operations.

  40. **one quart and one cup minus one pint equals**

    A. one quart and one cup

    B. one quart, one pint, and one cup

    C. one pint

    D. one pint and one cup

Answer: D

  41. **one gallon, three quarts, and 5 cups minus five quarts and two cups**

    A. one gallon, two quarts, three cups

    B. two quarts, three cups

    C. one gallon, three cups

    D. three cups

Answer: B

Rationale (40-41): The above subtraction operations depend upon the person knowing that two cups equal one pint, two pints equal one quart, and four quarts equal one gallon. Again, we work from the largest whole number of the larger units and express what is left over in the smaller units.

42. A car traveling north at 50 km/hr will be where 3 hours from now if 0 is the beginning point?

    A. 150 km north of 0

    B. 50 km north of 0

    C. 50 km from 0 heading north

    D. 1.5 km north of 0

Answer: A

Rationale (42): Distance equals rate or velocity times the length of time. So, the total number of kilometers (distance) equals the rate (50km/hr) times 3, the number of hours.

43. In the problem 12 divided by (-4) = c, the unknown "c" is equal to

    A. 4.8

    B. +3

    C. -3

    D. 48

Answer: C

Rationale (43): The rule here is that whenever we multiply or divide a plus by a minus, or the reverse, we get a negative integer for the answer.

44-46. Solve the following problem applying appropriate rules to the order in which arithmetic operations are performed.

44. [(6 - 2) X 4] + 1 = _____

   A. 16

   B. 17

   C. 23

   D. 20

Answer: B

45. [(2 - 3) X -4] + [6 X (2 - 1) + 3] = _____

   A. 13

   B. -13

   C. 18

   D. 28

Answer: A

46. [(3 - 5) X 7] + [(1 - 3) X (4 + 1)] = _____

   A. 15

   B. -13

   C. -28

   D. -15

Answer: C

Rationales (44-46): In all cases, we group terms from the inside out. Convert the contents of the parentheses ( ) into positive or negative integers, then solve for the contents of the square brackets[ ].

47. $(-3)^4$ means

   A.   -(3 X 3 X 3 X 3)

   B.   (3 X 3 X 3 X 3)

   C.   -(-3 X -3 X -3 X -3)

   D.   (-3) (-3) (-3) (-3)

Answer: D

Rationale (47): Minus 3 multiplied by itself 4 times is shown as (-3) (-3) (-3) (-3). This is the meaning of -3 to the fourth power.

48-49. For the English phrases given, which is the correct symbolic translation?

   48. The sum of n and a.

   A. n + a

   B. a - n

   C. an

   D. an

Answer: A

   49. The square of the difference of n and a.

   A. (n2 - a2)

   B. n - a2

   C. (n - a)2

   D. n - a

Answer: C

Rationales (48-49): The sum of n and a is simply shown as "n + a." The term difference indicates that "a" is subtracted from "n." A "2" denotes the squaring of "n - a" which is placed in parentheses.

50. If you multiply Jim's age by 4 and add 3, the result is 47. What is Jim's age?

    A. 47

    B. 10

    C. 11

    D. 19

Answer: C

Rationale (50): A product of 44 is derived by multiplying 11 by 4. Adding 3 more equals 47. To solve the problem as written, work backwards by subtracting first the 3 years, then dividing the ensuing 44 by four. The quotient is the answer.

51. Which is a "multiple" of 7?

    A. 300

    B. 343

    C. 1714

    D. 2371

Answer: B

Rationale (51): The number 7 divides equally into 343, and not into the other numbers. **Multiples** must come out in whole numbers, so in this case, 49 is the answer.

52. What is 1/2 of 3/4?

    A. 3/6

    B. 1/2

    C. 3/8

    D. 2/8

Answer: C

Rationale (52): Find 1/2 by raising 3/4 to the next highest common denominator which makes it 6/8. One-half of 6/8 is 3/8.

53. 1) A rectangle is a parallelogram with right angles.
    2) a rectangle has all of the properties of a parallelogram.
    3) All of the angles of a rectangle are right angles.
    4) A quadrilateral in which all of the angles are right angles is a
       rectangle.
    How many true statements are there defining a "rectangle?"

    A. 1

    B. 2

    C. 3

    D. 4

Answer: D

Rationale (53): A **rectangle** is a four-sided figure having four internal right angles. It therefore meets the definition of parallelogram, which is simply a four-sided figure whose opposed pairs of sides are parallel. And a quadrilateral is simply a figure with four straight lines joined at four corners.

54. Which of the following statements is not true?

    A. -8 + 12 = 4

    B. 8 - 12 = -4

    C. -8 + (-12) = -20

    D. 8 - (-12) = -20

Answer: D

Rationale (54): When we subtract a negative integer from a positive integer, the negative integer becomes a positive, and the answer to "d" is 20, not -20. When we combine (add) two negative integers, the result is the negative sum, seen in "c." The other two examples are simple addition and subtraction with opposed signs.

55. Which of these contains the correct "least common denominator?"

    A. $\dfrac{12 + 24 + 48}{6} = 7$

    B. $\dfrac{12 + 24 + 48}{12} = 7$

    C. $\dfrac{12 + 24 + 48}{24} = 7$

    D. $\dfrac{12 + 24 + 48}{7} = 7$

Answer: B

Rationale (55): The **least common denominator** is the largest number in the denominator which will divide evenly into all the numbers in the numerator. In "a," we used 6, which is not the largest number possible, so the correct answer here would be 14, not 7. In "c," 24 does not divide evenly into 12, so the answer would be 3 1/2, not 7. In "d," 7 does not divide evenly into any of the numbers in the numerator; so the answer here would be 12, not 7. In "b" we find that 12 is the largest number that will divide evenly into all three numbers of the numerator, and their sum is 7.

56. Which statement here is correct?

A. $2^2 + 2^3 = 10$

B. $2^2 + 2^3 = 12$

C. $2^2 + 2^3 = 32$

D. $2^2 + 2^3 = 9$

Answer: B

Rationale (56): In "b," we have squared 2, yielding 4; then we cubed 2, yielding 8; and the sum is 12. In "a," we have erroneously multiplied 2 by its exponents both times, yielding 4 and 6; the sum is 10. In "c," we have correctly squared the first 2 and cubed the second 2; then we erroneously multiplied 4 by 8 instead of taking the sum. In "d," we have erroneously added the numbers to their exponents.

57. One of these statements is true. Which is it?

A. $.3 + .0003 + .03 + .003 = 3.0009$

B. $.3 + .0003 + .03 + .003 = 0.3009$

C. $.3 + .0003 + .03 + .003 = 0.3333$

D. $.3 + .0003 + .03 + .003 = 3.3333$

Answer: C

Rationale (57): The easiest way to ensure doing this problem correctly is to line the numbers up vertically.

$$
\begin{array}{r}
.3000 \\
.0003 \\
.0300 \\
+\ \underline{.0030} \\
.3333
\end{array}
$$

All the wrong solutions are the result of mis-aligning the digits with respect to the decimal point, which is the common point to all the numbers.

58. Which of these is a negative integer?

    A. -4

    B. -.4

    C. 4

    D. -1/4

Answer: A

Rationale (58): An integer is a whole number, thereby eliminating "b" and "d." Answer "c" is a positive integer, while the integer in "a" carries the negative sign.

59. Here is a set of information given in a computation problem. "Jim has 9 oranges, Tom has 8 apples, and Pete has 7 pears." One of the following questions cannot be answered with the information provided. Which is it?

    A. What is the total amount of fruit owned by the three boys?

    B. What is the average number of pieces of fruit owned by the three boys?

    C. Which boy has the biggest piece of fruit?

    D. Which boy has the most pieces of fruit?

Answer: C

Rationale (59): The sum total of pieces of fruit ("a") is 24. The average number of pieces of fruit ("b") is 8. Jim has 9 pieces ("d"), the most. We have no information on the size of the fruit.

60. **A farmer needs to put up 8 sections of fence. How many posts will he need to hold up the fence?**

    A. 10, one per section, plus 2 extra for the ends

    B. 8, one post for each section

    C. 16, one for each end of each section

    D. 9, one for each section plus an extra for the loose end

Answer: D

Rationale (60): This problems lends itself to making a diagram. We need one post at the beginning of each section, and one extra one for the end of the eighth section.

Social Studies

1. **Which theorist became known in the field of curriculum development largely because of his controversial elementary social studies program, Man: A Course of Study (MACOS).**

    A. Jerome Bruner

    B. Jean Piaget

    C. Howard Gardner

    D. David Ausubel

Answer: A

Rationale (1): **Jerome Bruner's** ideas about children's learning have been considered to be controversial by some. Nevertheless, his thoughts as written in MACOS have had much influence on social studies curriculum. Bruner seems to have contributed a theory of instruction, thus taking teaching beyond a theory of learning.

2. **According to Bruner, "iconic representation" is a means of representing reality through imagery. This more advanced stage of learning seems to correspond most closely with which of Piaget's developmental stages?**

    A. Sensorimotor

    B. Intuitive or preoperational

    C. Concrete operations

    D. Formal operations

Answer: D

Rationale (2): **Iconic representation** (Bruner) is a means of representing reality through imagery; it is an advanced stage of learning. The icons provide our minds with mental images that become a reality. **Formal operations** (Piaget) is the abstract level of thinking. At this level, formal patterns of thinking and active symbolic processes are developed.

3. Which theorist purported educational goals that are universally thought of as "child- centered and humanistic?"

A. Jerome Bruner

B. Jean Piaget

C. Carl Rogers

D. David Ausubel

Answer: C

Rationale (3): Carl Rogers' educational goals, as stated in his book <u>Freedom to Learn</u> (1983), are considered to be child-centered and humanistic.

4. The type of intelligence that Howard Gardner describes as "the ability to access one's own feeling and to label, discriminate, and symbolize one's range of emotion in order to understand behavior" is

A. Personal intelligence

B. Kinesthetic intelligence

C. Spatial intelligence

D. Logical-mathematical intelligence

Answer: A

Rationale (4): Seven different "intelligences" have been described by Howard Gardner. These are in addition to what is usually thought of as comprising intelligence in a cognitive sense. They are: linguistic intelligence, musical intelligence, logical-mathematical intelligence, spacial intelligence, bodily kinesthetic intelligence, and personal intelligence. **Personal intelligence** is defined in two forms: intrapersonal and interpersonal. **Intrapersonal intelligence** is the ability to access one's own feelings and to label, discriminate, and symbolize one's range of emotional in order to understand behavior. **Interpersonal intelligence** involves the ability to make distinctions about other person's moods, temperaments, motivations, and intentions. The development of a sense of self is central to both.

5. **David Ausubel suggests that "discovery learning" is based on the idea that content must be discovered by learners before they can internalize it. In his thinking, this type of learning emphasizes**

   A. Product

   B. Process

Answer: B

Rationale (5): **Discovery learning** emphasizes the **process** of learning; whereas, **reception learning** emphasizes learning content as **product**.

6. **Which is UNTRUE regarding advance organizers?**

   A. They are considered to be useful tools in helping students to conceptualize the information they learn from books, films, lectures, and demonstrations.

   B. They are intended to be overviews of material to be learned given in advance of the learning.

   C. They are presented at a lower level of abstraction and inclusiveness than the learning task itself in order to build understanding of content.

   D. They are proposed by David Ausubel as a means of teaching through deductive learning.

Answer: C

Rationale (6): An **advance organizer** is a tool intended to help students conceptualize an overview of the material to be learned. Advance organizers are presented ahead of the learning task itself, and at a higher level of abstraction than the learning task.

7. Which of the following terms coined by anthropologists refer to the learning experiences a person has as a result of his or her culture?

    A. Acculturation

    B. Enculturation

    C. Tradition

    D. Diffusion

Answer: B

Rationale (7): Anthropologists have terms they use to define the conceptual structure of anthropology. These terms include, but are not limited to, acculturation, enculturation, tradition, and diffusion. The changes that result when two cultures make contact with one another is **acculturation**. Those learning experiences a person has as a result of his or her culture is **enculturation**. Customs and beliefs of a culture that are transmitted from one generation to succeeding generations is **tradition**. The flow of ideas, traits, and tools from one culture to another is **diffusion**.

8. _____ is the study of groups and the subsequent norms of behavior that human beings exhibit as a result of their group membership.

    A. Economics

    B. Geography

    C. History

    D. Sociology

    E. Political science

Answer: D

Rationale (8): **Economics** focuses on the production and consumption of goods and services. The basic concepts of **geography** are concepts of space. **History** encompasses past events as well as current events as they unfold and become history in all areas of human behavior. **Sociology** is the study of groups and the norms of behavior that are demonstrated by humans as a result of their group affiliation. Lastly, the attempt to analyze the relationships among people and institutions that make up political systems, and to determine the existence of these systems is referred to as **political science**.

9. **In which of the following teaching approaches is "citizenship" the key concept?**

   A. Child-centered

   B. Society-centered

   C. Knowledge-centered

Answer: B

Rationale (9): The **society-centered approach** is directed toward the development of involved, participating citizens. Thus, **citizenship** is the key concept of this approach.

10. **At which step in a lesson plan would you incorporate motivational activities to arouse students' attention?**

   A. Key idea

   B. Set

   C. Instruction

   D. Assessment

   E. Closure

Answer: B

Rationale (10): The basic components of a lesson plan are: key idea, instructional objective, set, instruction, assessment, and closure. At the stage of **set** the teacher wants to arouse students' attention and stimulate their imagination by incorporating motivating experiences and activities.

11. **Which skill refers to quantifying data, performing graphic analysis, mapping, making charts, and writing summaries.**

    A. Recording

    B. Data gathering

    C. Data processing

    D. Evaluating

Answer: C

Rationale (11): Skills that effective teachers will incorporate into their lessons include, but certainly are not limited to, recording, data gathering, data processing, and evaluating. **Data processing** includes quantifying data, performing graphic analysis, mapping, making charts, and writing summaries. **Recording** includes recalling information observances, photographing, mapping, drawing, illustrating, writing, tape recording, and listing. **Data gathering** specifies identifying and selecting data sources; determining appropriate methods; conducting surveys, historical studies, experiments, and interviews. **Evaluating** is making judgments and decisions, determining validity, and detecting errors and fallacies.

12. **Which skill includes "planning, producing, documenting, theorizing, and developing systems?"**

    A. Analyzing

    B. Synthesizing

    C. Predicting

    D. Hypothesizing

Answer: B

Rationale (12): The skills **synthesizing** includes "planning, producing, documenting, theorizing, and developing systems." **Analyzing** is "discriminating, categorizing, finding patterns, identifying attributes, and detecting structures." "Determining relationships, forecasting outcomes, and correlating variables" represent the skill **predicting**. **Hypothesizing** means "guessing in an educated way, developing hunches, and testing assumptions."

13. **Teacher presentation or lecture, class discussions, and demonstration lessons are strategies of which type of instruction?**

    A. Direct instruction

    B. Indirect instruction

Answer: A

Rationale (13): **Direct instruction**, or expository learning, is defined as the transmission of knowledge from a source to a receiver. Sources can be teachers, textbooks, films, lectures, tapes, trade books, and encyclopedias, while students are the receivers.

14. **A strategy included under "indirect instruction" that is designed to give learners the opportunity to be philosophical, that is to consider, discuss, and argue issues, is**

    A. Inquiry

    B. Role play

    C. Reflective thinking

    D. Differentiating assignments

Answer: C

Rationale (14): **Reflecting thinking** gives learners the opportunity to be philosophical, that is to consider, discuss, and argue issues. This type of thinking is applied to help students analyze tasks they have performed and speculate how things might happen under certain circumstances.

15. **An unobtrusive (i.e., does not interrupt instruction) alternative evaluation procedure allows a teacher to obtain from individual students a brief synthesis about what they think they have learned during a particular amount of time. To implement this procedure, the teacher merely stops what the class is doing and asks each student to list several things that he or she has learned during the activity. This procedure is called**

   A. An interview

   B. A spot check inventory

   C. An attitude scale

   D. Self-reporting

Answer: B

Rationale (15): The **spot check inventory** enables the teacher to find out from students what they think they have learned. Thoughts can be listed on the board from a group, or written privately by individuals and then shared with the group. Alternatives would be to have students write paragraphs, short stories, or use some other written forum.

16. **A characteristic of a formal essay test is which of the following?**

   A. It requires students to choose among several designated alternatives.

   B. It consists of many specific questions that require only brief answers.

   C. Students spend most of their time reading and thinking when taking the test.

   D. It affords much freedom for students to express their individuality.

Answer: D

Rationale (16): A **formal essay test** requires students to plan their answers and to express them in their own words. While doing so, it affords them the opportunity to express their individuality. Other characteristics of essays are: most of the test time is spent thinking and writing; these tests are easy to prepare but more time and effort is needed to grade them; these tests permit and often encourage bluffing by students; and grading is controlled by the grader, sometimes with uncertain criteria.

ELEMENTARY SAMPLE QUESTIONS

17. Which technique for changing the scale of a map would incorporate the use of an opaque projector to project the map on a wall for tracing.

    A. Mechanical method

    B. Optical method

    C. Mathematical method

Answer: C

Rationale (17): The **mathematical method** also called the method of similar squares, is useful for both enlargements and reductions. This is done by plotting points on a grid of larger or smaller dimensions, and then connecting them. Projecting the image using an opaque projector is one way of doing this.

18. Of the four types of inquiry research, which focuses on obtaining information or data about groups of persons?

    A. Historical research

    B. Descriptive research

    C. Survey research

    D. Experimental research

Answer: C

Rationale (18): **Surveys** are a way of gaining information about a group of persons. **Historical research** is an attempt to assimilate pieces of the past. **Descriptive research** focuses on the description of human behavior, primarily through observation. Lastly, **experimental research** involves the manipulation of variables using an experimental treatment group and a control group.

19. **Sometimes researchers live among tribal groups in order to make direct observations and to record human behaviors of these individuals. This method of investigation is known as**

   A. Participant observation

   B. Direct observation

   C. Indirect observation

   D. Interviewing informants

Answer: A

Rationale (19): "Descriptive research" focuses upon human behavior by primarily using observation. **Participant observation** is when the investigator participates within the group and observes it simultaneously. In **direct observation**, the researcher observes without being a participant. **Indirect observation** depends upon viewing existing data like pictures, artifacts, written accounts, books, maps, and so on. Tape recorders, cameras, and field notes are sometimes used to ensure accuracy. One obtains information by asking questions when engaged in the method of **interviewing informants**.

20. **The type of study that merely asks for people's opinions is**

   A. Descriptive

   B. Survey

   C. Historical

   D. Experimental

Answer: B

Rationale (B): In a **survey**, the researcher asks for people's opinions; whereas, in a **descriptive study**, a researcher describes people actually doing things.

21. **Which of the following exemplifies a stereotype, that is an oversimplified generalization about a particular group, race, or sex, that too often carries negative implications?**

    A. Illustrations of Native Americans portrayed as naked, arrow-shooting savages.

    B. Story lines where Caucasian behavior standards are needed for minorities to get ahead.

    C. Story lines where the achievements of women and girls are due to their good looks and their relationships with men.

    D. All of the above.

Answer: D

Rationale (21): All of the examples are **stereotypes**. The first two are about race and cultures, and the third, gender and roles.

22. **Which type of goal structure identified by Johnson and Johnson (1974) maintains that "one person can attain an individual goal only if others fail to obtain theirs."**

    A. Competitive

    B. Individualistic

    C. Cooperative

Answer: A

23. **A teacher plans an activity that teaches students "cooperative goal structure" when he or she**

   A. Places the students into groups and has each group compete with the others

   B. Keeps students in a large group and rewards the one who gets the most answers correct

   C. Arranges students into groups where they are encouraged to come up with answers by working together

   D. All of the above

Answer: c

Rationale (22 & 23): In a **competitive** situation, an individual can attain an individual goal only if others fail to obtain theirs. In an **individualistic** situation, each person's goal attainment is unrelated to the goal attainment of others, and each person is rewarded for his or her own achievement. Finally, in a **cooperative** learning environment, when one person achieves a goal, everyone else achieves their goal as well, because people help each other in an interactive way.

24. **A large classroom of students was divided into groups of 15. As Mrs. Jones circulated among the groups, she saw that about 5 or 6 of the students were enthusiastically engaged in discussion about the topic. It soon became obvious to Mrs. Jones that a "grouping problem" had occurred. Which one is it most likely to be?**

   A. An insufficient amount of time had been allotted.

   B. The task was vague and unclear.

   C. Too much time was given for the activity.

   D. The groups were of inappropriate size; they were too large for meaningful interaction by all members to occur.

Answer: D

25. **The Harvard laboratory study found that the larger the group size, the more likely**

   A. A few students will dominate while the others will withdraw or be reluctant to talk

   B. Group members will talk equal amounts of time

   C. All students will participate and offer input

Answer: A

Rationales (24 & 25): **Grouping** problems have been identified. They include: unclear group tasks; too much time which leads to group breakdown; inappropriate group assignments (i.e., better done individually); size, too few or too many; inadequate number of roles and activities; and teachers giving up on grouping too soon.

26. **The type of grouping that is done based on achievement or intelligence test scores is referred to as _____ grouping.**

   A. Age level

   B. Ability

   C. Interest

   D. Perceived needs

Answer: B

Rationale (26): Groups are formed based on various criteria. **Ability** groups are based on test scores. Groups are formed based on **age and grade level**. **Interests** sometimes contribute to groupings. Groups formed due to **perceived needs** can maximize the individuality of students.

27. **Interest centers, bulletin board that are integrated into class content, and student work on display are examples of which key factor to a teacher's social studies curriculum?**

    A. Goal structures

    B. Grouping patterns

    C. Physical setting

Answer: C

Rationale (27): The **physical** components of a learning environment are just as important as goal structures and grouping patterns. These components include: interest centers; furniture arrangement; private spaces for teachers and students; displays of student work; bulletin boards that highlight student work and provide learning prompts and teaching devices.

28. **Which is a characteristic of "divergent thinking" in contrast to convergent thinking?**

    A. Emphasis on learning the right answers

    B. Agreement sought in answering questions

    C. Answers based on students' ideas and research

    D. Answers that tend to give facts and explain systems

Answer: C

Rationale (28): **Divergent thinking** includes: a focus on developing one's own answers and constructing reasons for answers; answers based on students' ideas and research that tend to analyze and evaluate systems; participation in discussions for the purpose of disagreement and clarification of issues. Overall, divergent thinking requires and encourages original thinking.

29. **To which level of Bloom's Taxonomy does the descriptive question "Can students combine ideas" relate?**
    A. Comprehension
    B. Application
    C. Analysis
    D. Synthesis

Answer: D

30. **"Can students make judgments" is a question that corresponds with Bloom's level of**

    A. Knowledge

    B. Comprehension

    C. Application

    D. Evaluation

Answer: D

31. **When the teacher asks students to graph data using the bar graph method that they learned the week before, the teacher is essentially having students perform a task at which level of Bloom's Taxonomy?**

    A. Knowledge

    B. Comprehension

    C. Application

    D. Analysis

Answer: C

32. **Asking a student to tell "why" a fact is correct or incorrect helps to determine that student's level of**

   A. Comprehension

   B. Knowledge

   C. Evaluation

   D Application

Answer: A

Rationales (29, 30, 31, & 32): Teachers can encourage higher level thinking using a taxonomy like Bloom's. These levels of thinking can be identified by asking descriptive questions like the following:
1. Knowledge--can students recall information?
2. Comprehension--can students explain ideas?
3. Application--can students use ideas?
4. Analysis--do students see relationships?
5. Synthesis--can students combine ideas?
6. Evaluation--can students make judgments?
                    (Ellis, 1991, p. 267)

33. **A curriculum that involves "becoming a person" and "reaching my unique potential" is including opportunities for developing skills especially related to which value?**

   A. Pluralism

   B. Dignity

   C. Integrity

   D. Cooperation

Answer: C

Rationale (33): To some extent, values are taught within a social studies curriculum. **Integrity** means honesty, wholeness, and sincerity. "Trying my best" and "Becoming a person" help to teach integrity. **Pluralism** denotes a respect toward values of others, even though they are different. Teachers who show respect for each individual and expect their students to do the same toward each other helps to instill the value of **dignity**. Group projects, common goals, and interdependence foster **cooperation**.

ELEMENTARY SAMPLE QUESTIONS

34. At which of Lawrence Kholberg's levels of moral development is authority, fixed rules, and the maintenance of social order valued?

    A. Pre-conventional

    B. Conventional

    C. Post-conventional

Answer: B

35. Which of the following best epitomizes the post-conventional level on Kohlberg's hierarchy of moral development?

    A. The physical consequences of an action determine its goodness or badness

    B. Behavior is maintained in accordance with the expectations of the person's family, group, or nation, regardless of immediate or obvious consequences

    C. Right behavior occurs when one shows respect for authority, does one's duty, and maintains the social order for its own sake

    D. Right action is defined in terms of individual rights, and in terms of standards that have been examined and agreed upon by the whole society

Answer: D

Rationales (34 & 35): A hierarchical model for levels of moral development was designed by Lawrence Kohlberg. At the **preconventional** level the child obeys rules as "good" or "bad" based on reqards and punishments. At the **conventional** level, maintaining the expectations of the individual's family, group, or nation is perceived as important. The **postconventional** level stresses awareness of personal values and rights of others.

36. Multicultural education is NOT

A. An idea or concept

B. A "tack-on" to the school curriculum

C. An educational reform movement

D. A process

Answer: B

Rationale (36): **Multicultural education** is an idea or concept, an educational reform movement, and a process. It is an integral part of the curriculum--not a "tack-on."

37. All of the following statements are facts. Which one is an opinion of the writer?

A. Last Friday a political rally was held on the college campus.

B. The local newspaper and television station reported that approximately 2,000 people attended.

C. The mayor and other city officials were there.

D. All politicians are liars and crooks.

Answer: D

Rationale (37): Students obtain information from media sources like newspapers, magazines, television, radio, presentations, and word-of-mouth. Students need to be able to tell the difference between factual and opinion-oriented information. They are taught to do this by analyzing content and making decisions regarding fact and opinion.

38. **Which is LEAST helpful when designing opportunities for utilizing simulations in instruction?**

    A. Identify what objectives need to be fulfilled.

    B. Determine which elements of fantasy need to be included in the activity.

    C. Decide on the number of players who can participate and the roles they will play.

    D. Develop ways of reconstructing and analyzing the simulation activities.

Answer: B

Rationale (38): **Simulations** are attempts to represent and model reality through the medium of a game, role play, or some other physical activity. In order to develop a simulation, teachers must be mindful of several factors. These factors include: deciding on specific objectives, numbers of players and their roles, ways of analyzing and critiquing results. The teacher must determine which elements of "reality," not fantasy, need to be included.

39. **At which grade level is the chronological history of the United States typically studied?**

    A. Kindergarten

    B. Grade 3

    C. Grade 5

    D. Grade 6

Answer: C

40. When are students generally taught about the beginnings of the Western Civilization?

A. Kindergarten

B. Grade 3

C. Grade 5

D. Grade 6

Answer: D

Rationales (39 & 40): The social studies curriculum is designed to be taught in increments, or in a developmental sequence. For example, the chronological history of the United States is typically studied during the fifth grade, and the beginnings of Western Civilization during the sixth grade.

41. The 1781 Articles of Confederation were replaced by the U.S. Constitution of 1787 because:

A. Under the Articles of Confederation the central government was too powerful

B. The Articles of Confederation kept the 13 British colonies in North America subject to the British Parliament

C. The Articles of Confederation ceded huge territories to Britain in exchange for U.S. independence

D. The Articles of Confederation were so weak that the central government could not function as a nation-state

Answer: D

Rationale (41): The Articles of Confederation pleased the colonial leaders who feared a powerful central government. But the government thus created could not tax and legislate for legitimate purposes such as defense, postal services, and currency standardization, making it more truly a confederation of semi-sovereign nations instead of a country.

42. **The three biggest "real estate deals" that formed the modern United States after the Revolution for Independence were:**

    A. The Louisiana Purchase (*1803), the Treaty of Guadelup-Hidalgo (1848), and the Alaska Purchase (1867)

    B. The Treaty of Paris (1783), the Gadsden Purchase (1853), and the Morrill Land Grant Act (1862)

    C. The Treaty with Spain over Florida (1819), the Treaty with Britain over Oregon (1846), and the Annexation of Hawaii (1898)

    D. The "54^0 40' or Fight" dispute over Canada (1843), the Northwest Ordinance (1787), and Remon-Eisenhower Treaty over the Panama Canal (1977)

Answer: A

Rationale (42): The three treaties in answer "a" are the biggest land acquisitions done <u>after</u> the original United States' boundaries were set by the Treaty of Paris in 1783. The Morrill Act of 1862 reserved proceeds from the sale of certain public lands for education. All the other treaties named added smaller sections to the United States than those in answer "a."

43. **The division of powers in the U.S. government, as envisioned by the architects of the Constitution, are as follows**

    A. Executive, legislative, and fiscal powers

    B. Executive, legislative, and judicial powers

    C. Police, defense, and judicial powers

    D. Parliamentary, executive, and administrative powers

Answer: B

Rationale (43): James Madison wrote a strong defense for dividing governmental powers at each level into the **executive**, **legislative**, and **judicial** functions. The following are merely a sub-set of executive powers: fiscal, police, defense, and administrative. Parliamentary powers are legislative powers organized on the English model, where the chief executive is elected by the majority party within the legislative body.

44. **The U.S. Senate was envisioned by the founders of the United States as the higher of two legislative bodies. Which characteristics does it have?**

A. Four-year terms, initiation of money bills, control of foreign policy

B. Six-year terms, two members per state, confirmation power over treaties and presidential nominations

C. One member per 640,000 citizens, control over the news media, confirmation power over presidential elections

D. Six-year terms, one member per 640,000 citizens, veto power over the budget

Answer: B

Rationale (44): The Constitution provides two senators per state, while there is a legally fixed ratio between the population and the number of representatives in the House of Representatives (lower house). The lower house initiates money bills, while the Senate ratifies treaties and presidential appointments. Senators serve six-year terms. Both legislative houses may pass laws affecting the news media, but the 1st Amendment to the Constitution gives the media strong protection.

45. **The "federalist system of government" in the United States means:**

A. A delicately crafted balance of powers between the central government in Washington D.C. and the 50 states, which are the component parts

B. A one-party system headed up by George Washington's original political followers

C. That all true political authority is vested in Washington D.C., seat of the federal government

D. A book written by John Jay, James Madison, and Alexander Hamilton

Answer: A

Rationale (45): Our "federalist system" refers to the balance between the center and the component parts. We use the term "federal government" to refer to the national government in Washington D.C., which is confusing. George Washington's followers formed the now-defunct Federalist Party, which contended against the Republican party (Thomas Jefferson's followers) when the United States was born. A book called The Federalist Papers was assembled by Jay, Madison, and Hamilton to explain and help sell the federalist system to the public.

46. Which activity would not teach high school students to appreciate daily economic life in the 19th century (the 1800s)?

A. See an educational film comparing the <u>laissez-faire</u> economic principles of Adam Smith with Karl Marx's critique against capitalism.

B. Visit a reconstructed model agricultural community featuring live actors who recreate the farming activities of the 1870s, using the equipment and methods of the era.

C. See quality film set in the Civil War era, one in which the director paid heed to authentic detail of daily life.

D. Ask each student to interview a grandparent or other family elder about recollections of daily life as told by her/his own grandparents.

Answer: A

Rationale (46):   Economic theory does not teach the details of daily life. A quality film, carefully constructed interviews, or a visit to a functional museum of lifestyles can provide the cognitive information in memorable affective setting.

47. Which system for studying government would probably be the least effective for 7th graders?

A. Attending a governmental body meeting, with prior preparation on role and scope

B. Interviewing five adults about their views on government

C. Acting out a governmental body's role in making a decision

D. Memorizing a diagram with boxes for governmental units connected by solid lines showing authority, dotted lines showing coordination roles

Answer: D

Rationale (47): Cognitive memorization of governmental roles and functions is difficult because the learner has no set of pegs upon which to hang the information. Watching government in action, interviewing adults about their ideas, and role playing governmental functions all carry an affective dimension which allows the student to assemble facts upon a framework of meaning.

48. **Which would be the best way to explore the controversial Vietnam Conflict with 10th graders?**

   A. Have each student interview five veterans and turn in a report summarizing the interview.

   B. Require each student to read one book on the war and write a book report.

   C. Have the students read a short, objective survey of the main events, then design and carry out a balanced plan of interviews, press survey analysis, or book reports.

   D. Re-enact a heated confrontation between the war's supporters and its opponents.

Answer: C

Rationale (48):   Even though Vietnam veterans display a spectrum of views, they are still a skewed sample. Few full-length books on the Vietnam Conflict are balanced, and 10th graders do not have the historiographical sophistication to know the difference. Re-enactment of a confrontation would underline the emotional content but teach little about the real issues that were at stake. A short outline history will give the 10th grader a framework, and the colorful spectrum of opinion can then be captured by doing interviews, press surveys, or book reports.

49. **Which activity would not teach 9th grade students about the citizen's duty to support and participate in government?**

   A. Have a federal judge talk about the things an immigrant must learn and do to become naturalized citizen.

   B. Take the class for a tour of a fire station.

   C. Get the City Clerk to describe the roles of citizen advisory boards.

   D. Have the Supervisor of Elections describe the voting process, devoting attention to close outcomes and citizen turnout.

Answer: B

Rationale (49): While the Fire Department tour would undoubtedly discuss citizen duties regarding safety, the other three activities focus explicitly on what citizens do in the governmental sector.

ELEMENTARY SAMPLE QUESTIONS   80

50. Which activity would show 6th graders the most about municipal government?

    A. A short reading, followed by trips to city facilities and reports by the students on what they have seen

    B. Reading articles on several different cities

    C. Having the mayor or a city council member give a talk

    D. A visit to the Police Department

Answer: A

Rationale (50): A cognitive knowledge base followed by reinforcing affective/cognitive mixed experiences is the most complete. The other three choices all emphasize one aspect with minimum reinforcement.

51. Rivers carry soil downstream, depositing this sediment at the point where the river meets the sea. The built-up deposit becomes new land called

    A. An embankment

    B. A delta

    C. An inlet

    D. A tributary

Answer: B

Rationale (51): An **embankment** is a river's edge or shore, an inlet is a water-filled indentation in a coastline, and a tributary is a lesser river flowing out of a larger river.

52. Which of the following are not natural resources?

A. Sub-soil ore

B. Fish in coastal waters

C. Assembly plants

D. Forests

Answer: C

Rationale (52): **Assembly plants** are man-made and staffed. Ores, fish, and forests occur naturally.

53. An imaginary line connecting the highest points along a major mountain range is called

A. The continental shelf

B. The dew-point

C. The flood plane

D. The continental divide

Answer: D

Rationale (53): The offshore underwater land mass is the **continental shelf**. The dew-point is the temperature at which moisture condenses out of air. The flood plane is an arbitrary land elevation at which flooding occurs at certain intervals (e.g., 100 years, 50 years, 10 years, etc.). The **continental divide** separates the downhill flow of water into opposite directions.

54. A region with a heavy annual rainfall would be called

    A. Arid

    B. Tropical

    C. Temperate

    D. Jungle

Answer: B

Rationale (54): **Arid** is the term for extremely light annual rainfall. Temperate connotes a balanced rainfall favorable to agriculture. Tropical means a heavy rainfall, and jungle is the heavy natural growth found in some, not all, tropical regions.

55. The study of soils is called

    A. Agronomy

    B. Geology

    C. Agriculture

    D. Agricultural economics

Answer: A

Rationale (55): Agricultural economics relates all farm and forest products to the total economy. Agriculture itself is the production of crops and livestock. **Geology** is the study of the earth's surface, and **agronomy** is a sub-set that analyzes crop production capabilities of soils.

56. Which is true about socialism?

A. Large corporations operate the economy under close government control.

B. Secret police infiltrate the citizens' daily lives.

C. An aggressive foreign policy is a common feature.

D. The government owns the major means of production and distribution.

Answer: D

Rationale (56): Under fascism, the government operates the economy through government-controlled corporations. Secret police operate in many authoritarian and totalitarian governments; **socialism** is an economic system. Foreign policy under socialism ranges across the spectrum of passive to aggressive. The central trait is government ownership of the major means of production and distribution.

57. Neo-liberal economics are

A. A system of private entrepreneurs with government regulation and safety nets for select citizens.

B. Arbitrary governmental takeovers of previously private enterprises.

C. Social programs for the poor.

D. Elections pertaining to economic choices.

Answer: A

Rationale (57): **Neo liberalism** adds governmental regulation of critical economic sectors and safety nets for humane purposes to the older concept of free enterprise. Arbitrary governmental takeovers of the means of production occur under communism, fascism, and other kinds of dictatorship. Social programs for the poor are one aspect of new-liberalism. Neo-liberal economics pre-suppose democratic elections, but economic choices are only part of the total electoral process.

58. Communism is discredited in much of today's world. Which of the following was not one of its major leaders?

A. Lenin

B. Stalin

C. Marx

D. Hitler

Answer: D

Rationale (58): Lenin organized and led the Revolution of 1917 in Russia. Stalin took over the reigns of communism and led the Union of Socialist Republics from the 1930s into the 1950s. Karl Marx wrote Das Kapital and "Communist Manifesto of 1848," the most important intellectual supports for communism. Adolph Hitler led a fascist movement in Germany known as Nazism, proclaiming his strong opposition to communism.

59. Liberalism, in modern democratic governments, supports all but one of the following ideas.

A. Strongly graduated income tax

B. Minimal tax on corporate earnings

C. Government programs to assist the poor

D. Government programs to assist minorities based on quotas

Answer: B

Rationale (59): Modern **liberalism** uses the power of the national government to offset the inability of select individuals to succeed in a post-industrial society. Taxing the wealthy to finance continuing democratization and assistance for the less fortunate is an economic centerpiece.

60. Conservatism, in modern democratic governments, supports all but one of the following ideas.

A. Reduced taxation on corporations and capital gains

B. Mobilization of the poor through the "trickle down" of private investment into increased employment

C. Government controlled racial quotas for publicly support institutions of higher education

D. Private investment, rather than public foreign aid, to improve the economies of poor foreign countries

Answer: C

Rationale (60): Modern **conservatism** envisions minimal government interference in the flow of money, and stronger wages and employment as a result of jobs created by this process. This process has been called "trickle down." Consequently, lower taxation on corporations and private earnings on investments is a conservative platform. Similarly, private investment instead of public grants-in-aid is the conservative view on helping poor foreign countries. Racial quotas set by the government are in direct opposition to conservative philosophy.

Science

1. **It is reported that one in _____ males are at least partially color blind; whereas, only about one in _____ females have this problem.**

   A. 12, 200

   B. 10, 24

   C. 12, 24

   D. 10, 200

Answer: A

Rationale (1): In a typical classroom, there are more boys than girls who are color blind. Studies report that one male in 12 has the deficiency, contrasted with only one in 200 females.

2. **The part of the eye that regulates the amount of light entering the eye is the**

   A. Iris

   B. Pupil

   C. Lens

   D. Cornea

Answer: B

Rationale (2): The **iris** has a small hole in it called the **pupil**. The **pupil** regulates the amount of light entering the eye; whereas, the **iris** contains pigment that absorbs some colors and reflects others. The **lens** is a transparent, biconvex, and nearly spherical part of the eye that can change shapes in order to assist the eye with focusing on near and far objects. The **cornea** is the transparent part of the coat of the eyeball which covers the iris and the pupil and admits light.

3. An eye lens is more like which type of shape?

   A. Convex

   B. Concave

   C. Round

   D. Oval

Answer: A

Rationale (3): The eye lens is **convex** in shape; however, a muscle permits it to change shape in order to focus.

4. Which is true about "farsightedness?"

   A. The eyeball is longer

   B. The cornea or the lens may be thinner

   C. The image focuses in front of the retina rather than on it

Answer: B

Rationale (4): In **farsightedness**, the cornea or the lens may be thinner, or the eyeball shorter, than it normally occurs in order for an image to focus on the retina. In **nearsightness**, the cornea or the lens may be thicker, or the eyeball longer, than it normally occurs for perfect focusing of an image on the retina.

5. In which type of material are MOLECULES the closest together and relatively "fixed" in place?

A. Gas

B. Liquid

C. Solid

Answer: C

Rationale (5): There is some space between all molecules; however, in **solid** material, molecules are very close together and are relatively "fixed" in place. Molecules of most **liquids** are slightly farther apart. **Gas** molecules are widest apart. The cohesion is greater in solid states than it is in liquid or gas states. The lack of cohesiveness allows the liquid to take the shape of the container. Gases take the container's shape or escape from an uncovered container.

6. Molecules come almost to a standstill at absolute zero which is

A. -460° F

B. 212° F

C. 32° F

D. 0° F

Answer: A

Rationale (6): Molecules come almost to a standstill at absolute zero (-460° F or -273° C).

7. Water boils at

A. 0° C

B. 32° C

C. 39° C

D. 100° C

Answer: D

Rationale (7): Water boils at 100° C (212° F). A centigrade thermometer is divided into 100 parts or degrees, from freezing to boiling; a centigrade thermometer is also called a Celsius thermometer.

8. Of all solids, METALS are the best conductors of heat of all solids. Of the metals, which is the very best conductor?

A. Aluminum

B. Copper

C. Steel

D. Iron

Answer: B

Rationale (8): Metals are the best conductors of all solids; however, each type of metal varies in conductivity. The best conductor of solids is **copper**, followed by aluminum, steel, and iron.

9. The best cup for holding hot coffee is one made of _____ materials. This is because this type of solid material is a "poor" conductor of heat.

    A. Glass

    B. Plastic

    C. Ceramic

    D. Metal

Answer: C

Rationale (9): The best type of cup for holding any hot liquid is ceramic because this type of solid material is a poor conductor of heat.

10. Air temperature is warmest at what time of day due to the "greenhouse" effect?

    A. Mid-day

    B. Midmorning

    C. Afternoon

    D. Evening

Answer: C

Rationale (10): Air temperatures get warmest in the **afternoon** rather than at mid-day, or any other time, due to the "greenhouse" effect. Even though the sun is most nearly overhead at mid-day, the buildup of heat continues for several hours afterward.

11. **Light travels about _____ miles per second.**

    A. 10,000

    B. 86,000

    C. 100,000

    D. 186,000

Answer: D

Rationale (11): Light travels about 186,000 miles (297,000 kilometers) per second.

12. **Which condition affects the speed of sound?**

    A. Temperature

    B. Density

    C. Elasticity

    D. All of the above

Answer: D

Rationale (12): Three conditions affect the speed of sound: **temperature**, **density**, and the **elasticity** (i.e., springiness) of the molecules conducting the sound.

13. "Reverberations" occurs when

A. There is load sound

B. Loud sound can be carried a distance of at least 55 feet to and from our ears

C. Many distant reflecting surfaces produce multiple echoes

D. All of the above

Answer: D

Rationale (13): Multiple echoes of **reverberations** occur when there is the combination of a loud sound and many distant reflecting surfaces. Echoes can be heard when sound travels to the reflecting surface and back to our ears, a distance of at least 55 feet (6.5 meters) from the surface.

14. A magnet CAN NOT pick up things made of:

A. Steel

B. Iron

C. Copper

D. None of the above

Answer: C

Rationale (14): The best known metals attracted to a magnet are iron and steel. Less known, but also magnetic metals are cobalt and nickel. Common metals NOT attracted by magnets are brass, aluminum, tin, silver, stainless steel, copper, bronze, and gold.

15. If a person living in New York City were to suspend a bar magnet from a string, the magnet would point toward which magnetic pole?

    A. North

    B. South

Answer: A

Rationale (15): A bar magnet suspended from a string in any classroom in North America (including the United States, of course) will point toward the north magnetic pole. Likewise, the magnetic bar, if hung anywhere in South America, will point toward the south magnetic pole. This happens because like poles (north-north or south-south) repel each other. Opposite poles (south-north or north-south) attract each other.

16. Which is an UNTRUE statement about the earth and its magnetic field?

    A. The earth itself acts like a giant magnet.

    B. Several parts of the earth's interior rotate at different speeds.

    C. The earth's core is made up of nickel-iron which has the effect of being a huge electromagnetic buried within the earth.

    D. The north and south "magnetic poles" are the same as the north and south "geographic poles."

Answer: D

Rationale (16): The north and south "magnetic" poles are not the same as the north and south "geographic" poles. The magnetic and geographic poles are about 1,600 kilometers (1,000 miles) apart in the north and 2,400 kilometers (1,500 miles) apart in the south. Users of a compass, for example, find there is an angular variation between true north and the direction toward which a compass points as north.

17. All of the following are poor conductors of electricity, or insulators, except

A. Metals

B. Rubber

C. Glass

D. Plastic

E. Cloth

Answer: A

Rationale (17): The term **conductor** is given to any substance that permits an easy flow of electricity. Metals are the best conductors of electricity. Copper is commonly used as wires for this purpose. The term **nonconductor** is used for materials such as rubber, glass, plastic, cloth, and other nonmetallic substance.

18. The smallest bit of any substance that retains the chemical properties of that substance is called a(n)

A. Atom

B. Molecule

C. Electron

D. Proton

Answer: B

Rationale (18): Most matter is made up of molecules. In fact, a molecule is the smallest bit of any substance that retains the chemical properties of that substance. Subdividing a molecule produces substances at the atomic level. Atoms are composed of particles including electrons and protons.

19. The best example of a "lever" is a

A. Can opener

B. Paper cutter

C. Nail

D. Airplane propeller

Answer: A

Rationale (19): A **lever** is a bar used to expert a pressure, or sustain a weight, at one point of its length, by the application of a force at a second, and turning at a third on a fixed point called a "fulcrum."

20. Which is not an example of a "screw?"

A. A spiral staircase

B. An adjustable piano stool

C. The adjustable parts of a wrench

D. A pencil sharpener

Answer: D

Rationale (20): A **screw** is a common mechanical device that has an inclined plane with threads which are wrapped around a cylindrical shank in distances from each other called pitch. Examples of this device are nails, spiral staircases, roads that wind around a steep hill or mountain, vises for workbenches, clamps to hold things together, adjustable piano stools, and adjustable parts of wrenches.

21. The object that best represents a "straight-line motion" is a

    A. Merry-go-round

    B. Lawn mower

    C. Roller skate

    D. Swing

Answer: C

Rationale (21): Some machines have a **straight-line motion**. Examples include an upright bicycle, roller skates, steamrollers, and trains.

22. Friction enables a person to

    A. Brake a car or bicycle

    B. Walk or run

    C. Write on paper

    D. All of these

Answer: D

Rationale (22): **Friction** accompanies all motion. It is the resistance produced when two surfaces rub together. Sometimes friction lessens a machine's efficiency. Parts are more rapidly worn out and heat is created. In the more positive vein, friction allows us to brake a car or bicycle, walk or run, write on paper, and so on.

23. **"Germination" is a term that refers to**

    A. The swelling of a seed from moisture in the soil.

    B. The emerging root and stem from a seed.

    C. The penetration of a stem through the soil.

    D. The entire growth process, from seed to seedling.

Answer: D

Rationale (23): **Germination** is a term that encompasses the entire growth process from spore or seed to bud or plant.

24. **Dwarf ivy, fern, liverworts, and lichens are ideal plants for what type of terrarium?**

    A. Woodland

    B. Marsh

    C. Desert

Answer: A

Rationale (24): Different kinds of plants live in different habitats. Some ideal plants for a **woodland terrarium** are: dwarf ivy, ferns, liverworts, and lichens. Partridge berry and mosses provide a nice ground cover. Pebbles, sand, and bits of charcoal, mixed together, make for a good bottom layer of soil. The pebbles and sand provide drainage, and the charcoal absorbs gases and keeps the solid from turning sour. A second layer of moistened, rich garden soil, sand, and a bit of charcoal is recommended.

25. What substance enables a leaf to chemically combine carbon dioxide from air with water to form a simple sugar?

    A. Photosynthesis

    B. Carbon dioxide

    C. Chlorophyll

    D. Oxidation

Answer: C

Rationale (25): **Chlorophyll**, a green-pigmented chemical inside leaf cells, enables a leaf to chemically combine carbon dioxide from the air with water to form a simple sugar. **Photosynthesis** is the process of providing energy from sunlight to power the chemical synthesis in the leaf. **Carbon dioxide** is taken up from the air in **photosynthesis**, and **oxygen** is released as a waste product.

26. A bee obtains nectar from one flower and then carries it to another one. This is called

    A. Self-pollination

    B. Cross-pollination

Answer: B

Rationale (26): **Self-pollination** occurs when pollen from a flower's own stamens fertilize the ovules. **Cross-pollination** happens when pollen from one flower pollinates another flower.

27. Examples of fungi include

A. Mushrooms

B. Puffballs

C. Yeast

D. All of the above

Answer: D

Rationale (27): **Molds** are a subgroup of organisms classified as **fungi**. Other common examples of fungi include mushrooms, mildews, puffballs, and yeasts.

28. The statement that is true about molds is which? Molds

A. Manufacture the nutrients they need to live

B. Are most likely to thrive where it is light, dry, and cool

C. Include plants called fungi

D. Give off tiny, seed like spores which are found in the air almost anywhere

Answer: D

Rationale (28): Tiny, seed like spores from **molds** are in the air most everywhere. The spores settle on a variety of animal and plant materials, and on some synthetic materials on which molds grow. Unlike green plants, molds and fungi cannot manufacture their own food. They get the nutrients they need to live from the materials on which they grow. Molds may grow under a variety of conditions, but most often they thrive where it is dark, moist, and warm.

29. An example of a crustacean is a

    A. Crawfish

    B. Clam

    C. Snail

    D. Scorpion

Answer: A

Rationale (29): **Crustaceans** are animals without backbones (i.e., **invertebrates**). Examples include crayfish, crab, and lobster. The other animals listed are also invertebrates; however, clams and snails are mollusks, and a scorpion is an arachnid.

30. An animal with vertebrates is a

    A. Centipede

    B. Grasshopper

    C. Toad

    D. Starfish

Answer: C

Rationale (30): A toad is an example of an animal with a backbone or a **vertebrate**. It is an amphibian. The other animals are **invertebrates**: a centipede is a myriapod; a grasshopper is an arthropod; a starfish is an echinoderm.

31. Which class of vertebrates represents the lowest of the five classes?

    A. Birds

    B. Mammals

    C. Fishes

    D. Amphibians

    E. Reptiles

Answer: C

Rationale (31): Animals with backbones are, in descending order, mammals, birds, reptiles, amphibians, and fishes.

32. An example of a flesh eating carnivore is a

    A. Dog

    B. Horse

    C. Goat

    D. Raccoon

Answer: A

Rationale (32): Examples of flesh eaters (i.e., **carnivores**) are: cats, dogs, and seals. Horses and goats are plant eating **herbivorous** animals. Raccoons are **omnivorous** and eat both plants and other animals.

33. A bird that cannot fly is a

    A. Hawk

    B. Kiwi

    C. Woodpecker

    D. Woodthrush

Answer: B

Rationale (33): We ordinarily think of birds as fliers; however, chickens and road runners seldom fly, Some birds, like the ostrich, penguin, and kiwi, cannot fly at all.

34. _____ are cold-blooded animals.

    A. Mammals

    B. Birds

    C. Reptiles

Answer: C

Rationale (34): In contrast to warm-bloodied animals like mammals and birds, **reptiles** are **cold blooded**.

35. Frogs, toads, and salamanders are examples of an animal class called

    A. Reptiles

    B. Amphibians

    C. Fishes

Answer: B

Rationale (35): Frogs, toads, and salamanders are examples of an animal class called **amphibians**.

36. Which is UNTRUE about insects?

   A. They have eight jointed legs.

   B. The fly, moth, and grasshopper are examples of insects.

   C. They have an external skeleton made of a crusty substance called chitin.

   D. Each insect's body has three main parts: head, thorax, and abdomen.

Answer: A

Rationale (36): All insects have three pair, or **six jointed legs**, and an external skeleton made of a crusty substance called chitin. Each insect's body has three main parts: a head, a thorax, and an abdomen. The fly, moth, and grasshopper are examples of insects.

37. An ecosystem can be described as

   A. The connection between plants, plants eaters, and animal eaters.

   B. Relationships between a community and its physical environment.

   C. The specific environment or place where an animal or plant lives.

   D. Organisms that live and reproduce there.

Answer: B

Rationale (37): Animal and plant communities depend on interactions between each other and with the physical environment in general (e.g., air, water, enriched soil, temperature, and light). The sustaining of life through these interrelationships is called an **ecosystem**.

38. Marrow that is stored inside the middle of bones and mainly composed of fat is called

A. Red marrow

B. Yellow marrow

C. White marrow

D. Blue marrow

Answer: B

Rationale (38): A soft material called "marrow" is found inside many bones. There are two kinds of marrow: red marrow and yellow marrow. **Red marrow** is found at the ends of bones where red blood cells are manufactured. **Yellow marrow** is mainly composed of fat and is stored in the middle of bones.

39. Which is NOT a true fact about tendons?

A. Muscles are attached to bone and cartilage by tendons.

B. Tendons are tough, white, twisted fibers of different lengths.

C. Tendons are enclosed in sleeves of thin tissue that contain a slippery liquid.

D. Tendons can only pull; they work in opposite pairs.

Answer: D

Rationale (39): **Tendons** are tough, white, twisted fibers that help to attach muscles to bone and cartilage. They are of differing lengths. Some are cord like while others are wider and flat. Tendons are enclosed in sleeves of thin tissue that contain a slippery liquid, enabling them to slide back and forth without rubbing. They are un-stretchable and very strong.

40. What is the solid material in plasma that helps to make the blood clot at the place where the body is injured and bleeding.

    A. Red cells

    B. White cells

    C. Platelets

Answer: C

Rationale (40): The liquid part of blood is called **plasma**. Three kinds of solid materials are found in plasma: red cells, white cells, and platelets. **Platelets** help the blood to clot whenever bleeding and bodily injury occur.

41. Foods that provide the principal source of energy to the body are rich in carbohydrates and _____

    A. Fats

    B. Proteins

    C. Vitamins

    D. Minerals

Answer: A

Rationale (41): **Carbohydrates** and **fats** in foods provide our main source of **energy**. Proteins are needed for growth and repair of body cells. Vitamins help regulate cell activities. Minerals also help regulate cell activities, and some are incorporated into body tissue.

42. The organic matter that supplies plants with nitrogen, phosphorus, potassium, and other essential elements is called

    A. Loam

    B. Humus

    C. Magma

    D. Silt

Answer: B

Rationale (42): **Humus** is the organic matter that supplies plants with nitrogen, phosphorus, potassium, and other essential elements. Magma is fiery molten rock found deep underground. This material, if it erupts through cracks in the earth's surface, is called lava. Silt is loose sedimentary rock particles found suspended in water. Loam is a soil consisting of a friable mixture of varying proportions of clay, sand, and organic matter.

43. Which type of rock is formed when pure limestone, shale, and sandstone are subjected to intense heat and pressure?

    A. Igneous

    B. Sedimentary

    C. Metamorphic

Answer: C

Rationale (43): **Metamorphic rocks** like marble, slate, and quartzite are formed when pure limestone, shale, and sandstone, respectively, are subjected to intense heat and pressure.

44. _____ water is the main source of evaporating water on earth.

   A. Lake

   B. Ocean

   C. River

   D. Rain

Answer: B

Rationale (44): **Ocean water** is the earth's main source of evaporating water, this it is the basic source for fresh water. This is because when the salty ocean water evaporates, the salt is left behind. Air currents carry water vapor inland. Here it condenses and falls as rain, hail, or snow, supplying water for rivers, streams, and lakes.

45. All of the following are true facts about oxygen EXCEPT which one?

   A. It makes up about 21 percent of the air.

   B. It combines readily with sugars in body cells and releases heat energy.

   C. It is needed for photosynthesis in green plants.

   D. It is necessary in order to burn materials.

Answer: C

46. Air is composed the LEAST of which gas?

A. Oxygen

B. Nitrogen

C. Carbon dioxide

Answer: C

Rationales (45 & 46): The air we breathe is composed of separate and distinct gases, the major ones being oxygen, nitrogen, and carbon dioxide. Nitrogen makes up about 78 percent of the air, with a lesser amount, 21 percent, oxygen. Oxygen combines with sugars in our body cells and releases heat energy. It is also necessary for any externalized burning of materials. Nitrogen is essential for plant growth, and dilutes the air we breathe. **Carbon dioxide**, only about 3/100 of 1 percent, is needed for photosynthesis in green plants.

47. The temperature at which condensation takes place is called the

A. Relative humidity

B. Dew point

C. Evaporation level

Answer: B

Rationale (47): The temperature at which **condensation** takes place is called the **dew point**.

48. When the gravitational attraction between the moon and the earth is at its greatest,

A. The more distance there will be between these two bodies.

B. The more likely a lunar eclipse will occur.

C. The higher the probability a direct high tide will occur.

D. The higher the probability an indirect tide will occur.

Answer: C

Rationale (48): The less distance between the moon and the earth, the greater the gravitational attraction between these two bodies and the higher the probability a direct high tide will occur.

49. The closest planet to the sun is

A. Venus

B. Mercury

C. Earth

D. Mars

Answer: B

Rationale (49): The planets which are the closest to the farthest in order from the sun are: Mercury, Venus, Earth, Mars, Jupiter, Saturn, Uranus, Neptune, and Pluto. An exception occurs when Neptune and Pluto cross paths and Neptune becomes the farthest planet from the sun.

Physical Education and Health

1. Which is a characteristic of a youngster with a mesomorph body type?

    A. Predominance of muscle and bone

    B. Performs poorly in aerobic and anaerobic skill-oriented activities

    C. Is considered to be stocky or obese

    D. Is thin

Answer: A

2. Earlier physically maturing children, heavier and tall for their age, are more apt to be of a (an) _____ body type.

    A. Mesomorph

    B. Ectomorph

    C. Endomorph

Answer: C

Rationale (1 & 2): Sheldon, Dupertuis, and McDermott (1954) developed the original scheme for identifying body types. These types were called **endomorphy**, **mesomorphy**, and **ectomorphy**. Children characterized as having a **mesomorph** body type have a large amount of muscle and bone. These youngsters usually perform well in team sports activities. **Ectomorphs** are thin and do well in aerobic endurance activities like jogging and track and field. Youngsters with **endomorph** physiques are soft and round, and some are obese. They do not do as well in physical performance as the other two classifications of body types.

3. Body composition refers to the varying amounts of what within the body?

    A. Muscle

    B. Bone

    C. Fat

    D. All of these

Rationale (3): **Body composition** is determined by the varying amounts of muscle, bone, and fat within the body.

4. During which of the learning phases in Fitts and Posner's (1967) motor skills developmental sequence does the learner receive ongoing feedback, eliminate errors, and begin to make necessary adjustments?

    A. Introductory phase

    B. Practice or motor phase

    C. Consolidation or autonomous phase

Answer: B

Rationale (4): This model helps to explain how motor skills are learned. The **introductory** or cognitive phase is first. The second phase is the **practice** phase during which it is essential that new skills be developed correctly. The final phase involves using the skills **automatically** in active settings.

5. **Identify the concept of mechanical principles in skill performance which describes "a measure of the push or pull that one object or body applies to another."**

    A. Stability

    B. Force

    C. Leverage and motion

Answer: B

Rationale (5): An understanding of mechanical principles is necessary for the effective performance of movement skills. **Stability** reflects balance and equilibrium, required in many athletic skills. **Force** is a measure of the push or pull that one object or body applies to another. **Body levers** are necessary to project force into motion. With the appropriate leverage, less effort is needed to accomplish the motion.

6. **"Roll over as large an area as possible to absorb the impact." This is a mechanical principle that describes what to do with the body to best accomplish the starting and stopping of body movements associated with**

    A. Ready position

    B. Fast starts

    C. Absorbing force

    D. Falling

Answer: D

Rationale (6): Mechanical principles can be applied to starting and stopping the body in most any activity in which they might be involved. Children must be taught to **fall** in order to be hurt as little as possible. They should be taught to roll over as large an area as possible to spread and to absorb the impact. They should also know that tucking the head and doing a forward or judo roll helps.

7. Which monitoring technique is put into action when the teacher asks students to pair up and evaluate each other's performance using a teacher-designed instrument.

A. Hand signals

B. Class check

C. Peer check

D. Written feedback

Answer: C

Rationale (7): The monitoring technique of **peer check** requires that students pair off and evaluate each other's performance using a teacher-designed instrument. More than one evaluation will help assure the validity of the score received.

8. Which is an example of the Premack Principle?

A. "You may shoot baskets (preferred activity) after you complete the passing drill."

B. "You may shoot baskets (preferred activity) now and then do passing drills."

C. "You may shoot baskets all period today."

D. "You cannot shoot baskets today."

Answer: A

Rationale (8): The **Premack Principle** is based on the motivating effectiveness of following a low interest activity with a high interest activity. In this example, the students are directed to complete the low interest activity (passing drill) before moving on the high interest or preferred activity (shooting baskets).

9. **Which is NOT an effective strategy to use to decrease undesirable behavior?**

    A. Identify the undesirable behavior, state why it is unacceptable, and tell students what behavior is desired.

    B. Reprimand the offending student in private.

    C. Tell the student that he or she is unacceptable.

    D. Redirect the student and reinforce his or her appropriate behavior when it occurs.

Answer: C

Rationale (9): All of the suggestions are effective strategies to use to decrease undesirable behavior except that the offending student should be told that his or her **behavior** is offensive and should stop. In other words, accept and child but not the behavior.

10. **Which is the MOST restrictive physical education placement option?**

    A. Regular physical education classes.

    B. Regular physical education classes with restricted class size.

    C. Regular physical education classes with an aide or classroom teacher support.

    D. Regular physical education classes plus part-time special education classes.

Answer: D

Rationale (10): Physical education placement options are listed from least to most restrictive in the selection given. Two more options proceeding in an even more restrictive direction are: full-time special education class and full-time physical education in school for special-education students.

11. Relays are useful for all EXCEPT

A. Enhancing cooperative skills

B. Following rules

C. Learning motor skills

D. Working toward common goals

Answer: C

Rationale (11): Students enhance cooperative skills because of the peer interaction during relay activities. While involved in relays, students must follow rules and directions. The focus for relay activities is on the outcome or common goal. Relays should utilize motor skills that are <u>already learned</u>.

12. Which is TRUE about intramural programs?

A. They should be the nucleus of a physical education program.

B. Children should be competitively selected to play on intramural teams.

C. Since this is a program "outside" the school curriculum, it is not important for the school community to make a commitment.

D. An intramural program offers students an opportunity to build interest and skills in a wide range of recreational activities.

Answer: D

Rationale (12): The **intramural program** should grow out of and be an extension of the physical education program. Its purpose is to provide a competitive recreational program that serves all children. The primary requirement for a functional intramural program is commitment by the school community. This commitment is based on recognition of the program's potential value for the students involved. An intramural program offers students an opportunity to develop interest and skills in a wide range of recreational activities. It also gives students an opportunity to develop and maintain a reasonable level of fitness.

13. A "maneuver" in basketball that protects the player's possession of the ball by keeping the body between the ball and the opposing player is called

  A. Pivoting

  B. Feinting

  C. Stopping

  D. Defending

Answer: A

Rationale (13): During a **pivoting maneuver**, the ball is held firmly in both hands with elbows out to protect it. The lead foot may step in any direction, but the pivot foot must remain in contact with the floor, even as that foot turns.

14. A simple "underhand toss" of a football to a teammate is called

  A. A lateral pass

  B. A forward pass

  C. Handing off the ball

  D. Centering

Answer: A

Rationale (14): In football, a simple **underhand toss** of a football to a teammate is called a **lateral pass**. The ball must be tossed side ward or backward, with easy motion, to qualify as a lateral pass.

15. **In hockey, the term _____ refers to stopping the ball and controlling it.**

    A. Tackling

    B. Fielding

    C. Dodging

    D. Passing

Answer: B

Rationale (15): The term **fielding** refers to stopping the ball and controlling it. Fielding the ball in hockey is as important as catching and controlling the ball in basketball.

16. **Which is a "defensive skill" that is taught in deference to "offensive skills?"**

    A. Passing

    B. Controlling

    C. Jockeying

    D. Volleying

Answer: C

Rationale (16): Knowing when to and when not to make a move to take possession of the ball is essential. Sometimes defenders must **jockey** until defensive support appears. **Jockeying** means to stay in close (i.e., one to two yards of the ball) in order to pressure the advancing player.

17. **Studying the origins of terminology used in physical education, such as "gymnasium," "calisthenics," and "exercise" integrates which of the following subject areas into physical education?**

    A. Music

    B. Language arts

    C. Mathematics

    D. Geography

Answer: B

Rationale (17): Sometimes selected academic skills and information can be learned better through physical activity. Thus physical education offers opportunities for integrating subject areas and physical activity. Studying the origins of terminology used in physical education integrates **language arts** with physical education. In addition, the world of sports is "ripe" with topics for written and oral expression.

18. **Which body movement is considered to be "rhythmic?"**

    A. Swinging a tennis racket

    B. Wielding a hammer

    C. Throwing a ball

    D. All are considered to be rhythmic

Answer: D

Rationale (18): ALL body movements tend to be **rhythmic**. Most movements that take place in physical education classes contain physical components.

19. _____ is a "non-locomotor skill" where the center of gravity is fluidly and gradually transferred from one body part to another.

   A. Bending

   B. Twisting

   C. Rocking

   D. Stretching

Answer: C

Rationale (19): When rocking, the body is in a rounded position where the floor is touched. The center of gravity is fluidly and gradually transferred from one body part to another during this **non-locomotor skill**.

20. Propelling the body up and down on the same foot describes the "locomotor skill" of _____ .

   A. Sliding

   B. Hopping

   C. Galloping

   D. Skipping

Answer: B

Rationale (20): **Locomotor skills** move the body from one place to another, or project the body upward, as in jumping or hopping. Other **locomotor skills** are walking, running, skipping, leaping, sliding, and galloping. Large muscle movement and gross motor coordination are involved.

21. **The physical fitness variable in "FIT" that uses heart rate in prescribing workouts is**

    A. Frequency

    B. Intensity

    C. Time

Answer: B

Rationale (21): The variable **intensity** utilizes heart rate in prescribing workouts. Students should acquire knowledge of basic fitness principles and the ability to apply them to a personal fitness program. Variables they need to know include: frequency, intensity, and time. Progression, mode of activity, specificity of exercise, and isotonics, isometrics, and isokinetics should also be understood.

22. **The majority of exercises used for physical fitness routines involve _____ contractions.**

    A. Isotonics

    B. Isometrics

    C. Isokinetics

Answer: A

Rationale (22): **Isotonic** contractions involve using a muscle through its full range of motion. Walking, jogging, calisthenics, and bicycling are examples of activities that utilize **isotonic** contractions.

Art, Music, and the Humanities

1. **The term graphic arts refers to all of the following EXCEPT**

   A. Use of crayons

   B. Use of chalk

   C. Use of paint

   D. Creation of sculpture

Answer: D

Rationale (1): **Graphic arts** utilizes crayons, chalk, paint, and pencils. The term **visual arts** refers to graphic arts and the creation of sculpture or collage.

2. **According to Lowenfeld and Brittain (1982), children begin to make attempts to represent objects that are familiar in their environment at about four years of age, which is also the beginning of the _____ stage.**

   A. Scribbling

   B. Pre-schematic

   C. Schematic

   D. Drawing realism

Answer: B

3. **Student art work during the stage of drawing realism is characterized by all EXCEPT**

   A. Smaller drawings

   B. More detailed drawings

   C. Eagerness to share drawings with adults

   D. Begins at about age nine

Answer: C

Rationale (2 & 3): Lowenfeld and Brittain (1982) identified four stages in children's drawings: scribbling, pre-schematic stage, schematic stage, and drawing realism. **Scribbling** begins at about thirteen months of age with the first scribbles appearing as zigzags. Distinct shapes like circles appear in their drawings at about three years of age. At about four years of age, the **pre-schematic** stage begins and is characterized by children making attempts to represent objects in their environments, or other drawings from their experiences. The **schematic** stage begins at about seven years of age. Definite forms representing the child's environment are drawn over and over. Figures are placed on a baseline and not at random. The stage of **drawing realism** is begun at around nine years of age. Drawings are smaller, more detailed, and not always shared with adults.

4. **Results of Brittain's (1969) study found ALL BUT which to be true about the ability of nursery school children to draw squares?**

   A. They must be trained.

   B. After "training" experiences with squares, children began to draw them at around four years of age.

   C. Children who were not taught "square making skills" were able to accomplish this task at the age of four.

   D. All are true facts.

Answer: A

Rationale (4): Results of this study reported that children were able to draw squares around the age of four whether they had pre-exposure or training, or did so naturally.

5. Which is a true statement about art in deference to crafts?

A. Something is produced.

B. Products are unique and different.

C. Outcome is predetermined.

D. Self-expression is not deemed very important.

Answer: B

Rationale (5): **Art** gives students the opportunity to explore media with no external product goals. The process of creating is more important than the result. **Craft** activities require that something be produced, with most of the products the same or similar when completed. **Art** incorporates planning, decision making, and self-expression; craft outcomes are predetermined.

6. Which materials are LEAST likely to be used when making collages?

A. Tissue paper

B. Natural materials

C. Paste and glue

D. Magic markers

Answer: D

Rationale (6): **Magic markers** are very useful in "graphic arts." Materials used in "collages" include: tissue paper; natural materials like seeds, leaves, tree bark; and materials found in the environment like buttons, ribbons, and so on.

7. Which is NOT a part of the resolution passed by the National Education Association (NEA, 1990)?

A. Artistic expression is basic to an individual's intellectual, aesthetic, and emotional development.

B. Fine arts transcend cultural barriers and foster multicultural understanding.

C. The belief that every elementary and secondary school curriculum must include a balanced, comprehensive, and sequential program of fine arts.

D. All are statements in the resolution.

Answer: D

Rationale (7): The main points of the resolution passed by the NEA in 1990 include: (a) artistic expression is basic to an individual's intellectual, aesthetic, and emotional development; (b) fine arts transcend cultural barriers and foster multicultural understanding; and (c) the belief that every elementary and secondary school curriculum must include a balanced, comprehensive, and sequential program of fine arts. Therefore, the correct answer is "d" as all are statements in the resolution.

8. Which is NOT an appropriate goal for a music program?

A. To expose children to a wide variety of types of music.

B. To teach children to sing solos.

C. To encourage children to experiment with tempo, volume, and quality of sound, along with opportunities to listen to music.

Answer: B

Rationale (8): All are appropriate goals for a music program except that children should be taught to sing "tunefully" according to a pattern of notes written on a musical score. Solos are fine for children who have natural, melodic voices and are motivated to learn to sing alone.

9. **Studies show that children learn songs in a pattern that is predictable and begins with _____.**

   A. Words

   B. Rhythms

   C. Phrases

   D. Contour

Answer: A

Rationale (9): Children learn songs in a predictable pattern that begins with **words** and moves to rhythms, phrases, and contour.

10. **When selecting songs to teach to young children, which is NOT point to consider? Songs should**

   A. Be appealing to children

   B. Have words that children understand

   C. Lend themselves to movement

   D. Avoid repetition

Answer: D

Rationale (10): All of the criteria listed, with the exception of avoiding repetition, should be considered when selecting songs to teach to young children. Conversely, repetition is important, along with shorter lyrics, and predictable patterns within each verse.

11. **Which is a "folk song" that is considered a good choice for teaching children?**

    A. "This Land Is Your Land"

    B. Songs from the movie "Mary Poppins"

    C. "Twinkle, Twinkle Little Star"

    D. "Where Is Thumpkin?"

Answer: A

Rationale (11): The folk song is "This Land Is Your Land." Nursery songs are "Twinkle, Twinkle Little Star" and "Where Is Thumpkin?" Popular songs from other cultures include songs from the movie "Mary Poppins."

12. **A child typically begins to "dance" to music with a marked rhythm at**

    A. Birth

    B. 1 to 2 years of age

    C. 2 to 3 years of age

    D. 3 to 4 years of age

Answer: C

Rationale (12): Toddlers seem to like a marked rhythm; thus, they will **dance** to this type of music in particular by bending the knees in a pounding motion, turning circles, swaying, swinging arms, and nodding the head.

13. Children generally begin to explore and seek out musical sounds at age

A. 4 to 8 months

B. 10 to 18 months

C. 18 months to 2 years

D. Two to three years

Answer: C

Rationale (13): Children demonstrate a preference for certain kinds of music by rocking, swaying hips, or clapping to songs they like. Displeasure is shown toward music they do not like by fussing, whining, escaping from the environment, and making distressed facial expressions.

14. An approach to musical instruction for young children that "combines learning music, movement, singing, and exploration" is

A. Dalcroze Eurthythmics

B. The Kodaly Method

C. The Orff Approach

D. Education Through Music (ETM)

Answer: D

Rationale (14): Of the four approaches to musical instruction for young children listed, the **Education Through Music approach** combines learning music, movement, singing, and exploration. The Dalcroze Eurthythmics approach is based on an awareness of music through body movement. The Kodaly Method relies on children's games, nursery songs, and folk music to help children learn to sing. Lastly, the Orff Approach involves structuring a musical environment and having children improvise through rhythm, body percussion (stamping, slapping the thighs, clapping, and finger snapping), dramatic movement, melody, and the use of both percussion and pitched instruments.

15. Psychodrama was originally developed for _____ purposes.

A. Therapeutic

B. Musical

C. Recreational

D. Artistic

Answer: A

Rationale (15): Psychodrama was originally developed for **therapeutic** purposes. Psychodrama and role playing techniques have been incorporated into several affective education programs concerned primarily with clarification of values and standards.

16. The chromatic scale has twelve half-tones, but when played as the standard octave it has seven jumps, two of them half-tones and the other five full tones. This is called

A. A symphony

B. A cadenza

C. Bach's organ fugue

D. Guido's scale

Answer: D

Rationale (16): **Guido** was an 11th century monk who is credited with "standardizing the scale." A symphony is an 18th century European musical form employing the different kinds of instruments in harmony. A cadenza is a run of notes played rapidly on the piano, and a Bach organ fugue is a stylized organ composition made famous by the German composer J. S. Bach.

17. The most purely authentic form of music that was invented within and is native to the United States is

A. The chorale

B. Rock

C. Jazz

D. Marching band

Answer: C

Rationale (17): The **chorale** began as a European blend of human voices, usually on a religious theme. **Rock** is claimed by the Europeans in the 1960s, often identified with England's Beatles. **Jazz** is purely an African-American art form, originating in New Orleans. **Marching bands** began in 19th century Europe.

18. Most of the world's music is a combination of two variables:

A. Chords and duration

B. Melody and rhythm

C. Strings and horns

D. Voices and wind instruments

Answer: B

Rationale (18): Virtually all the world's music is a series of notes at different pitches (the **melody**), spaced according to a plan (the **rhythm**). Chords are combinations of notes played together. Strings, horns, voices and winds are all instruments for making music.

19. Which statement about opera is false?

A. All the music was written prior to 1720.

B. It features singers supported by an orchestra, and sometimes by dancers.

C. The songs tell a story.

D. The singers appear in solos, combinations such as duets and trios, and in chorus.

Answer: A

Rationale (19): Operas were written in the baroque era (1600-1750), the classical era (1750-1820), and the romantic era (1820-1920). The songs tell a story and are done as solos and in combinations. An orchestra is usual; occasionally there are dancers.

20. Which of these activities would not encourage elementary scholars to learn music?

A. Have them sing a familiar song as a group.

B. Give the children rhythm sticks and have them tap the beat while they listen to a song.

C. Have each one try to play a tune on the piano while the others wait their turn.

D. Take them to hear a high school band practice some marching songs.

Answer: C

Rationale (20): Most children are not embarrassed to sing a familiar song, and very little instruction will enable them to tap the rhythm with sticks. High school bands have a rousing effect, and the children can role model upon the high school musicians. Most children cannot pick out a tune on a piano keyboard, and waiting in line will produce frustration and misbehavior.

21. **Plastic arts are**

    A. Painting, sculpture, woodcarving, and other art forms which employ solid, permanent materials

    B. Sculpted plastic figures in modernistic shapes

    C. Copies of enduring museum works

    D. Polymers and polyesters

Answer: A

Rationale (21): Plastic arts are tactile and use durable materials. The artistic beauty is created by color, shape, composition, surface, and lighting. Plastic itself is just one of these materials. Museum works can be copied on many materials. Polymers are structural materials, and polyesters are fibers.

22. **The following masterpiece was not created by the Florentine (Italian) artist Michelangelo (1745-1564):**

    A. The statue of David

    B. The painting Mona Lisa

    C. The Sistine Chapel ceiling paintings

    D. The tombs of Julius II and the Medici

Answer: B

Rationale (22): Mona Lisa was painted by another Italian Renaissance artist, Leornardo da Vinci. He and Michelangelo are often called the world's most important artists. David is the prototype for many statues of the human figure, the Sistine Chapel paintings are often termed the best Biblical art, and Michelangelo's famous tombs are combination of architecture and painting.

23. Which statement is true about impressionistic art?

    A. The figures look exactly as they appear in real life, hence the term "impression."

    B. It is an old Greek form designed to please the gods.

    C. The figures are approximations of their real life appearance, sometimes with deliberate distortions or lack of clarity.

    D. The art form consists of deep depressions into a clay surface.

Answer: C

Rationale (23): In the late 1800s, French painters like Claude Monet and P. A. Renoir thought that pictorial art was too controlled, too much like "picture postcards" for tourists. They evolved a style of painting that omits precise details, includes a thematic distortion, and aims at sending the viewer an interpretive message.

24. Frank Lloyd Wright's functional school of architecture stressed

    A. Harmony of the structure with nature, no artificial adornments, and ease of use by the occupant

    B. Precise geometric shapes

    C. Soaring vertical lines designed to conserve ground space

    D. Preservation of classical lines and support columns

Answer: A

Rationale (24): F. L. Wright tried to harmonize his structures with their setting, eliminating all artificial decoration. "User friendly" in an era when "good architecture" stressed European or classical form over convenience, Wright's structures are the proto-types of modern architecture.

25. The following is not a good activity to encourage 5th graders' artistic creativity:

A. Ask them to make a decorative card for a family member.

B. Have them work as a team to decorate a large wall display.

C. Ask them to copy a drawing from a book, with the higher grades being awarded to those students who come closest to the model.

D. Have each student try to create an outdoor scene with crayons, giving them a choice of scenery.

Answer: C

Rationale (25): Forcing a student to copy someone else's image may reveal a lack of hand-eye coordination or pictorial visualization, which decreases learning interest. Connecting creativity to thoughts about a family member or a favorite scene encourage a child to try. Group art work encourages social skills and heightens awareness of talent within the group.

PROFESSIONAL KNOWLEDGE
<u>**Child Growth and Development**</u>

1. The largest proportion of children (approximately 75 percent) with intellectual disabilities (mental retardation) are in the _____ category.

  A. Mild

  B. Moderate

  C. Severe

  D. Profound

Answer: A

Rationale (1): Severity levels of mental retardation (MR) are mild, moderate, severe, and profound. The largest proportion of youth with MR is in the mild range and estimated to be approximately 75 to 87 percent of the MR population. The next largest is at the moderate range, with 12 to 25 percent. The fewest number is in the severe and profound range of 6 to 12 percent (Ramsey, 1995).

2. Which is NOT a characteristic of learning disabilities?

  A. There is a discrepancy between a child's potential and his or her performance.

  B. There are generally specific subjects and areas in which a youngster is unable to do something that other classmates do quite easily.

  C. The condition is often evident in disorders of listening, thinking, talking, reading, writing, spelling, or arithmetic.

  D. The problems associated with a youngster's learning disability is the result of other problems relating to hearing, vision, or physical impairments.

Answer: D

Rationale (2): In the "exclusion clause" of the definition for learning disabilities, it is stated that the problem cannot be due primarily because of hearing, sight, or physical impairments. In other words, a youngster cannot be eligible for special education services of learning disabilities if he or she cannot achieve academically because of being unable to hear, see, or physically maneuver.

3. **Of the following infant temperament types identified by Thomas, Chess, and Birch (1968), which might be described as "low activity level; slow adaptation to change; somewhat negative mood; moderate or low intensity of reactions to stimulation."**

   A. Easy

   B. Difficult

   C. Slow to warm up

   D. Unclassified

Answer: C

Rationale (3): The child with an **easy** temperament is characterized as adaptable in sleeping, eating, and temperament. The child with a **difficult** temperament is slow to adapt to change, sleeps and eats poorly, and is negative in mood. The **slow to warm up** child shows irregularity in sleep and eating, is slow to adapt to change, withdraws from the unfamiliar, and is sometimes negative in mood. Varying mixtures of these characteristics are unable to be classified.

4. **Mrs. Jones, the kindergarten teacher, has noticed that Jamie cries when her mother brings her to school and leaves her in the classroom; but, rather than welcome her mother's return, Jamie appears angry. In fact, Mrs. Jones has seen Jamie push her mother away when she later returned to get her. According to the classification scheme by Ainsworth, which type of infant attachment is Jamie demonstrating?**

   A. Securely Attached

   B. Insecure-Avoidant

   C. Insecure-Ambivalent

   D. Disorganized/Disoriented

Answer: C

Rationale (4): Mary Ainsworth classified mother-infant attachments. The **securely attached** child uses mother as a base for exploration. **Insecurely attached** children display negative behaviors toward the mother during reunion. **Insecure-Avoidant** children "avoid" or ignore the mother's reentrance. **Insecure-ambivalent** children are upset when mother returns. Disorganized, disoriented children display any of a range of disorganized or disoriented behaviors.

5. **A child is considered to be developmentally delayed when he or she is incapable of performing a task of which _____ percent of children of the same age are capable.**

   A. 10

   B. 50

   C. 75

   D. 90

Answer: D

Rationale (5): A child is considered to be **developmentally delayed** when he or she is incapable of performing a task at which 90 percent of children of the same age are capable.

6. **Which is a child typically able to do at 2 years of age?**

   A. Climb stairs with help (two feet on each stair)

   B. Push/pull wagon

   C. Dress self using buttons, zippers, laces, and so on

   D. Roller skate

Answer: A

Rationale (6): Along with other physical and motor skills, a child at 2 years of age begins to climb stairs with help. At 4 years of age, the child is able to push and pull a wagon, and dress him or herself using buttons, zippers, laces, and so on. The ability to roller skate typically begins at age 5.

7. **Compensatory preschool programs are designed to make up for initial deficits in a child's early learning environment. The best known and most massive compensatory education program ever undertaken in the United States is Project Head Start. Which is "true" about this program? It was**

   A. Begun in 1950

   B. Conceived as part of the American war on poverty

   C. Begun in an attempt to end segregation

   D. Effective, but short-lived due to budgetary constraints

Answer: B

Rationale (7): Begun in 1964, Head Start was conceived as part of the American war on poverty. Lee and associates (1988) found that Head Start programs, contrary to original hopes, did not eliminate the differences between Head Start and comparison groups, but they did "reduce" this desparity. The program continues to be funded at the present time.

8. **Which is NOT true of the Montessori method, a much used approach to early intervention? It**

   A. Is solely a preschool program

   B. Dates back to the turn of the century

   C. Was initially developed for use with children with mental retardation

   D. Features the use of specially developed materials for teaching sense discrimination

Answer: A

Rationale (8): The Montessori method dates back to the turn of the century. Though initially developed for use with children with mental retardation, it has proven effective as a general program. It is designed for use not only in preschool, but in elementary and high school as well.

9. **Laura is an English-speaking high school student who plans to spend the summer in France in a language immersion program. Lambert refers to this situation as**

   A. Subtractive bilingualism

   B. Addictive bilingualism

   C. Transitional bilingualism

Answer: B

Rationale (9): W. E. Lambert (1975) describes **addictive bilingualism** as a situation in which learning a second language has a positive influence on the first language. **Subtractive bilingualism** imputes the negative influence of a second language. **Transitional bilingualism** is used to describe the common situation in which the dominant language replaces the minority language in a few generations.

10. **When two children say something like, "You be the teacher, and I'll be the student," they are engaging in what Parten has described as**

   A. Solitary play

   B. Parallel play

   C. Associative play

   D. Cooperative play

Answer: D

Rationale (10): M. B. Parten (1932) describes the play behavior of preschoolers as being solitary or as reflecting one of five different kinds of social play. **Cooperative play** is when children help one another in activities that require shared goals or a division of goals.

11. **A parent says to his or her youngster, "You seem to need help in structuring your telephone time with your friends; therefore, we must ask you to end your evening calls by 8 o'clock." This is an example of which parenting style?**

    A. Permissive

    B. Authoritarian

    C. Authoritative

Answer: C

Rationale (11): **Authoritative** parenting is somewhere between **permissive** and **authoritarian**. Firm control and obedience are descriptive words; however, it encourages rational discussion of standards and expectations. In the end, authoritative parenting tries to promote independence.

12. **To extend material or add something to it to make it more memorable is more descriptive of which type of process involved in long-term memory?**

    A. Rehearsing

    B. Elaborating

    C. Organizing

Answer: B

Rationale (12): There are three processes involved in the act of remembering: **elaborating**, **rehearsing**, and **organizing**. To **elaborate** is to extend material or to add something to it to make it more memorable. **Rehearsing** is repeating material and **organizing** is grouping and making relationships.

13. **Which is a sub-test on the Weschler Intelligence Scale for Children - Revised (WISC-R) that measures verbal rather than performance abilities?**

    A. Similarities (Child indicates how certain things are alike)

    B. Picture completion (Child indicates what is missing in pictures)

    C. Object assembly (Puzzles are assembled by subjects)

    D. Coding (Child pairs symbols with digits following a key)

Answer: A

Rationale (13): The sub-tests of the WISC-R that measure verbal performance abilities are: similarities, general information, general comprehension, arithmetic, vocabulary, and digit span.

14. **Which is a true fact about intelligence quotients (IQs)?**

    A. IQ is a constant

    B. IQ tests are fair measures of all the important things

    C. IQ tests are fair

    D. IQ is related to academic and job success

Answer: D

Rationale (14): An **intelligence quotient** is frequently misunderstood. It is NOT a score of innate intelligence, but it is an indicator, or predictor, of academic and job success.

15. Larry is always out there in the hallways talking with classmates as they change classes. Some of his peers like him a lot, while others do not particularly like him or feel they don't know him very well. Larry is probably an example of which category of social status, according to Gottman?

    A. Sociometric stars

    B. Mixers

    C. Teacher negatives

    D. Tuned out

    E. Sociometric rejectees

Answer: B

Rationale (15): J. M. Gottman (1977) identified five categories of social status of students. **Sociometric stars** are especially well-liked by their peers. **Mixers** have high peer interaction, with some well-liked and others not. **Teacher negatives** typically have conflicts with teachers. Some are well-liked by their peers and some are not. **Tuned out** describes students who are not involved with their peers, and are ignored rather than rejected. **Sociometric rejectees** are not liked very much by peers, and are more rejected than ignored.

16. Mary attributes her good grades to her teacher's assigning "easy" work. This is an example of attributing success to an _____ focus of control.

    A. Internal

    B. External

Answer: B

Rationale (16): **Learned helplessness** is a term that describes those persons who are more likely to attribute successes and failures to circumstances over which they have no control, thus this is referred to as having an **external locus of control**. Those with an **internal locus of control** attribute their effort, hard work, and self-discipline to their successes.

17. **Continually shaming or ridiculing a child, or depriving him or her of comfort or appropriate contact is most descriptive of which type of child abuse?**

   A. Physical abuse

   B. Physical neglect

   C. Emotional abuse

   D. Sexual abuse

Answer: C

Rationale (17): Not all maltreatment of children involves physical violence. Other forms of abuse are: physical neglect, emotional abuse, and sexual abuse. **Emotional abuse**, sometimes called psychological abuse, consists of behaviors that cause emotional or psychological harm to children. Continual shaming, ridiculing, isolating, confining them to small areas, blaming, yelling, severely verbally abusing them, or depriving them of emotional contact and comfort constitutes **emotional abuse**.

18. **Which term describes developmental changes that are relatively independent of the environment and more closely related to heredity?**

   A. Maturation

   B. Learning

   C. Growth

Answer: A

Rationale (18): To develop is to grow, to mature, and to learn. **Maturation** describes changes that are relatively independent of the environment and closely related to heredity. **Growth** refers to physical changes and **learning** results from experiences, not simply maturation or growth.

Developmental Psychology

1. A _____ study observes the same subjects over a period of time; a _____ study compares different subjects of different developmental levels at the same time.

    A. Longitudinal, cross-sectional

    B. Cross-sectional, longitudinal

Answer: A

Rationale (1): A **longitudinal** study is conducted over an extended period of time; therefore, the researcher observes the same subjects over this period of time. A **cross-sectional** study is conducted for a shorter length of time and compares several subjects at the same time.

2. According to Freud's theory, the _____, acts as a buffer between the instinctual drive and one's conscience, which are often in conflict with each other.

    A. Id

    B. Superego

    C. Ego

Answer: C

Rationale (2): Sigmund Freud contended that human development and behavior is reflected in three aspects of personality: **id**, **ego**, and **superego**. The **ego** acknowledges what is reality and acts as a buffer between the instinctual drive of the **id** and one's conscience which is called the **superego**.

3. During which developmental phase does the child need to interact with and be accepted by peers?

A. Trust versus Mistrust

B. Autonomy versus Shame and Doubt

C. Initiative versus Guilt

D. Industry versus Inferiority

Answer: D

Rationale (3): Erik Erikson developed a **psychological** theory in which he describes human development in eight stages. Interaction with and acceptance by peers is important during the **Industry versus Inferiority** developmental stage, which is his fourth stage.

4. Bandura's social-learning theory is based upon

A. Behaviorism (reward and punishment)

B. Observational learning (imitation)

C. Cognitive theory (thoughts and symbolizing)

D. Physiological aspects (body functions)

Answer: B

Rationale (4): Albert Bandura combined elements of behaviorism and cognitivism into a social-learning theory that is based upon **observational learning** or **imitation**. The theory contends that much human learning and behavior is a function of observing and imitating the behavior of models.

5. MaryAnne learned in school that all insects have six legs. One day, MaryAnne watched a spider crawl across the porch step on which she was sitting. Upon counting the spider's legs and finding a total of eight, MaryAnne quickly realized that a spider could not be classified as an "insect." That thought process is what Piaget calls

A. Assimilation

B. Accommodation

Answer: B

Rationale (5): Jean Piaget recognized the importance of structuring thinking in order to learn. According to this theory, each person approaches the learning task with an existing cognitive structure (or schemata). With **assimilation**, learners incorporate new experiences into their already existing cognitive structure. With **accommodation**, learners focus on the new features of a learning task, thereby changing or modifying their cognitive structures.

6. Jim was shown two glasses of water--one a tall, thin glass and the other a short, wide glass. Even though the latter glass appeared to have more water in it, upon measuring the contents, it was evident that the amounts of liquid in each glass were the same. Understanding "conservation" occurs during what Piaget defined as

A. Formal operations

B. Concrete operations

C. Preoperational thinking

D. Sensorimotor period

Answer: C

Rationale (6): The **preoperational thought**, or intuitive thinking level occurs during ages 5 to 7. During this cognitive developmental stage, the child begins to understand **conservation** of amount, quantity, number, and weight.

7. Which is not true about children with Down Syndrome? It

A. Is closely related to parental age

B. Is the most common chromosomal birth defect

C. Is often associated with mental retardation

D. Affects all children the same

Answer: D

Rationale (7): **Down Syndrome** is the most common chromosomal birth defect, affecting about one out of every 680 live births (Lefrancois, 1996). Mental retardation is common among children with this defect. It is closely related to older parental ages. Not all children are affected the same; varying degrees of the disorder may occur.

8. The fetal diagnosis, or assessment of an unborn fetus' development, that allows the physician to "see" the fetus and to obtain samples of tissues (and blood) from the fetus itself, is called

A. Amniocentesis

B. Ultrasound

C. Fetoscopy

D. Chronic vullus biopsy (CVS)

Answer: C

Rationale (8): The fetal diagnosis that allows the physician to see the unborn fetus and to obtain samples of tissues and blood from the fetus itself is called **fetoscopy**.

Language Development

1. Of the following abilities, which is generally expected of a student who is beginning kindergarten?

   A. Makes no misarticulations of sounds when saying a basic core of words.

   B. Writes stories independently.

   C. Uses relationship words such as "because" or "so."

   D. Uses abstract words discriminately and selectively.

Answer: C

Rationale (1): A child beginning kindergarten generally is able to use relationship words such as "because" or "so." At this age, a child asks "why," "how," and "what for" questions. There is an understanding of comparatives like "fast," "faster," and "fastest." Complex sentences and intelligible speech, with some mispronunciations, are the norm.

2. Preschooler James substitutes the "w" sound for the "r" sound when pronouncing words; therefore, he often says "wat" for "rat," and "wabbit" for "rabbit." His misarticulation is basically a disorder in

   A. Phonology

   B. Morphology

   C. Syntax

   D. Semantics

   E. Pragmatics

Answer: A

Rationale (2): **Phonemes** are the smallest units of sounds in words. It is common for preschoolers to substitute consonants like the "w" sound. This is generally outgrown as children begin school--by age six for girls and age 7 for boys.

3. _____ is a set of rules for relating words, phrases, and clauses to one another in forming sentences.

    A. Phonology

    B. Morphology

    C. Syntax

    D. Semantics

    E. Pragmatics

Answer: c

Rationale (3): **Syntax** is a set of rules for relating words, phrases, and clauses to one another when forming sentences. The typical child begins with one-word sentences during the first year and by age 3, shows mastery of the basic relationships between subject predicate and object.

4. Which is the study of the relationships between words and grammatical forms in a language and their underlying meaning?

    A. Phonology

    B. Morphology

    C. Syntax

    D. Semantics

    E. Pragmatics

Answer: D

Rationale (4): **Semantics** is the study of the relationships between words and grammatical forms in a language and their underlying meaning. Semantics involves language "content;" whereas, phonology, morphology, and syntax are concerned with the "form" of language.

5. **A set of linguistic features (syntactic, semantic, and phonetic) that allows mutually intelligible communication within a group of speakers defines the term _____.**

   A. Language

   B. Communication

   C. Semantics

   D. Pragmatic

Answer: A

Rationale (5): There are over 3,000 different **languages** spoken today. Two speakers are said to speak different languages when they unable to understand each other.

6. **An infant says "lala" everytime he wants his blanket. This preverbal vocalization is called a(an)**

   A. Telegraphic utterance

   B. Echolalia

   C. Protoword

   D. Deictic term

Answer: C

Rationale (6): A **protoword** is a sequence of sounds used by a child that has a relatively consistent meaning, but is not based on any adult word.

7. **When the child says "That doggie," meaning "That is the doggie," he or she is using speech called a**

   A. Telegraphic utterance

   B. Echolalia

   C. Protoword

   D. Deictic term

Answer: A

Rationale (7): Speech that consists of content words, with functions left out, sounds like a telegram. The correct answer is "a," a **telegraphic utterance**.

8. **One characteristic of autism is that these youngsters often repeat the speech of others. This speech characteristic is known as**

   A. Telegraphic utterance

   B. Echolalia

   C. Protoword

   D. Deictic term

Answer: B

Rationale (8): The act of repeating language heard in the speech of others is called **echolalia**; therefore, the correct answer is "b." (Words that are used as linguistic pointers like "here" and "there" are known as deictic terms).

9. **Children utter their first meaningful word somewhere between ages**

    A. Birth to 6 months

    B. 6 months to one year

    C. 12 months to 18 months

    D. 18 months to two years

Answer: B

Rationale (9): The first meaningful word spoken by a child occurs somewhere after six months of age and close to the child's first birthdays.

10. **Two-word sentences generally include modifiers which are joined to topic words to form declarative, question, negative, and imperative structures. Which is an "imperative utterance?"**

    A. "Pretty cat."

    B. "Where Daddy?"

    C. "Dog allgone."

    D. "More drink."

Answer: D

Rationale (10): Somewhere during their second year most children progress to stage of two-word combinations. They ask for more of something (**imperative**); they say no to something (**negative**); they make a statement (**declarative**); or they ask about something (**question**). Answer "d" states a request or makes a two-word command.

Special Education Characteristics

1. **An educational characteristic common to students with mild intellectual, learning, and behavioral disabilities is that they generally**

    A. Show interest in school.

    B. Have intact listening in classroom instruction.

    C. Require modifications in classroom instruction.

    D. Respond better to passive than to active learning tasks.

Answer: C

Rationale (1): Students with mild intellectual, learning, behavioral disabilities require **modifications** in classroom instruction. They also have other educational, psychological, and social characteristics in common.

2. **A characteristic found in common to children with moderate to severe intellectual disabilities is**

    A. The condition surfaces when learning demands are made

    B. Their physical appearance is the same as that of students in full-time regular classrooms

    C. There is an identifiable cause or etiology

    D. The development of poor self-concept

Answer: C

Rationale (2): In general, students with more **severe** disabilities are detected at birth and have known etiologies. Appearance is often different from those with mild, and no discernible, disabilities.

3. **Mike's teacher complains that he is constantly out of his seat. She also reports that he has trouble paying attention to what is going on in class for more than a couple of minutes at a time. His writing is often illegible, containing a great many reversals of letters and special problems. Although he seems to want to please, he is very impulsive and stays in trouble with his teacher. He is failing reading, and his math grades, though somewhat better, are still below average. Mike's psychometric evaluation should include assessment for**

   A. Mild mental retardation

   B. Specific learning disabilities

   C. Mild behavior disorders

   D. Hearing impairments

Answer: B

Rationale (3): Individuals with specific learning disabilities frequently are distractible and have trouble paying attention or focusing. Coordination difficulties may contribute to illegible handwriting, letter reversals, and spacing problems. Intra-individual discrepancies show uneven development between areas of functioning, like reading and math.

4. **Which is an attention problem that a student with a learning disability might exhibit?**

   A. Lack of selective attention

   B. Does not seem to consider consequences before acting

   C. Unable to control own actions or destiny

   D. Poor fine motor coordination

Answer: A

Rationale (4): Disorders of **attention** include: lack of selective attention, short attention span, inability to focus on one thing at a time, distractibility, and perseveration.

5. **In general, characteristics of students with learning disabilities include**

   A. A low level of performance in a majority of academic skill areas

   B. Limited cognitive ability

   C. A uniform pattern of academic development

   D. A discrepancy between ability and achievement

Answer: D

Rationale (5): A **discrepancy** between one's ability (potential) and actual achievement (performance) is a major characteristic of students with learning disabilities. In comparison, students with intellectual disabilities (mental retardation) generally demonstrate limited cognitive ability across academic subject and skill areas. Their performance shows a somewhat delayed, uniform pattern of academic development.

6. **A youngster with intellectual disabilities who appears clumsy and possesses poor social awareness, but who can be taught to communicate and to perform semi-skilled jobs under supervision is more than likely classified at which level of severity?**

   A. Mild

   B. Moderate

   C. Severe

   D. Profound

Answer: B

Rationale (6): Students with **moderate** intellectual disabilities share characteristics of: fair motor development, clumsy; poor social awareness; can be taught to communicate; can learn from supervised training in social and vocational skills; can perform semi-skilled jobs as adults.

7. **Which is LEAST true about students with an emotional/behavioral disorder?**

   A. Are assessed to have a high intelligence quotient (IQ)

   B. Display poor social skills

   C. Have discrepancies in academic achievement

   D. Possess a poor sense of personal identity

Answer: A

Rationale (7): Most students with an emotional/behavioral disorder display poor or inappropriate social skills, possess a poor sense of personal identity, and have discrepancies in academic achievement. Most score lower on tests of intelligence than their actual potential because their emotional or behavioral problems interfere with their testing.

8. **Which behavior would be expected at the mild level of emotional/behavioral disorders?**

   A. Inappropriate affect

   B. Self-injurious

   C. Poor sense of identity

   D. Attention seeking

Answer: D

Rationale (8): **Attention seeking** is expected at the **mild** level of emotional/behavioral disorders. Inappropriate affect, self-injurious behaviors, and poor sense of identity are among characteristics that are more identifiable of students with severe emotional/behavioral disorders.

9. Which of the following is a language disorder?

A. Articulation problems

B. Stuttering

C. Aphasia

D. Excessive nasality

Rationale (9): **Language disorders** have different origins and causes than speech disorders. Characteristics of language disorders include: difficulty in comprehending questions, commands, or statements; inability to adequately express one's own thoughts; language that is below the level expected for the youngster's chronological age; interrupted language development; qualitatively different language; and total absence of language called **aphasia**.

10. Which of the following is a speech disorder?

A. Disfluency

B. Aphasia

C. Delayed language

D. Comprehension difficulties

Answer: A

Rationale (10): Children with **speech disorders** are characterized by one or more of the following: speech-flow or **disfluency** disorders; unintelligible speech, speech that is difficult to understand, or articulation problems; unusual voice quality; peculiar physical mannerisms when speaking; obvious emotional discomfort when trying to communicate; or damage to nerves or brain centers which control muscles used in speech.

11. **Terry's teacher says that he is extremely shy and avoids social contact. Terry often appears inattentive, and seems to have difficulty carrying out directions that have been given verbally. The teacher also states that he has observed Terry having difficulty keeping his place when the class is reading out loud. Terry frequently misses school because of chronic earaches. Terry is demonstrating characteristics typical of students with a**

    A. Behavior disorder

    B. Hearing impairment

    C. Learning disability

    D. Intellectual disability

Answer: B

Rationale (11): Among other characteristics, students with **hearing impairments** often appear: inattentive; shy and avoiding of social contacts; unable to carry out verbal directions; have difficulty keeping the right place during verbal or choral reading. Physical symptoms like ear infections, history of middle ear complications like otitis media, fluid running from the ears, chronic allergies, sinus congestion, and others are sometimes indicative of a hearing problem as well.

12. **Frances complains of frequent headaches. She also loses her place during reading, squints, rubs her eyes frequently, and walks to the chalkboard to see what her teacher, Mrs. Marsh, has written. She should be referred for a(an)**

    A. Reading test

    B. Intelligence test

    C. Learning disability evaluation

    D. Visual screening

Answer: D

Rationale (12): Students with **visual impairments** often demonstrate similar symptoms to those recorded about Frances. They may lose their place while reading and confuse similarly appearing words, but these are indicators of a visual rather than a reading problem. Squinting, rubbing one's eyes excessively, and moving closer to written work are all characteristics of visual problems.

ELEMENTARY SAMPLE QUESTIONS

13. **Of the following characteristics, which is most related to neurological impairments?**

    A. Impaired motor abilities

    B. Lack of physical stamina

    C. Progressive weakening of muscles

    D. Side effects from treatment

Answer: A

Rationale (13): Students with physical disabilities sometimes have neurological impairments which can affect sensory abilities, cognitive functions, emotional responsiveness, and **impaired motor abilities**. Physical impairments can also affect the cardiopulmonary system and the musculoskeletal system. Students with any type of physical disability or health impairment often experience a lack of physical stamina, progressive weakening of muscles, pain or discomfort, physical limitations, and so on. Embarrassing side effects may occur form certain diseases or treatment.

14. **Muscular dystrophy is a condition that affects which of the three major systems of the body?**

    A. Cardiopulmonary

    B. Musculoskeletal

    C. Neurological

Answer: B

Rationale (14): Muscular Dystrophy is a disease that primarily affects the **musculoskeletal** system (i.e., muscles, bones, joints) of the body. Ultimately, the other systems are affected as muscles supporting them degenerate.

15. Which is TRUE about children with multiple disabilities?

A. The characteristics of children with multiple disabilities are determined by the types of combined disabling conditions.

B. Some children with multiple disabilities may exhibit self-injurious behavior,
    while others show appropriate social skills.

C. Children with multiple disabilities frequently possess intellectual and/or sensory impairments.

D. All of the above facts are true.

Answer: D

Rationale (15): Children who have **multiple disabilities** are a very heterogeneous population. Their characteristics are determined by the type and severity of their combined disabilities, thus they differ in their sensory, motor, social, and cognitive abilities. Although "any number or combination of disabilities is possible, major dimensions typically include mental retardation, neurological impairments, emotional disturbance, or deafness and blindness" (Ramsey, 1995, p. 53).

16. Children begin to demonstrate characteristics of giftedness

A. At a very early age

B. When interacting with preschool peers

C. During kindergarten and first grade

D. As adults in professional careers

Answer: A

Rationale (16): Giftedness may not be detectable at birth, but becomes apparent at an **early age**. Children with gifted abilities tend to demonstrate mental and physical superiority as preschoolers. They often display a keen curiosity, possess unusual knowledge and quick wit, and make associations readily. These youngsters come from all socioeconomic levels.

17. Traumatic brain injury is

    A. Included under the exceptionality category of Specific Learning Disabilities

    B. Largely a preventable condition

    C. Always fatal

    D. A leading cause of death for adults ages 30 to 50

Answer: B

Rationale (17): Like Autism, **Traumatic Brain Injury** became a separate special education exceptionality category under IDEA (the Individuals with Disability Education Act) in 1990. Brain injuries are largely preventable, with proper use of seat belts in vehicles, preventive medical care, appropriate adult supervision, and parent education. The leading cause of this type injury is motor vehicle accidents, with child abuse, falls, and high fever as the other most frequent contributors. It is not always fatal, but is a leading cause of death in persons under thirty-four years of age.

18. Students with attention deficit disorders (ADD) must be given needed special accommodations in the regular classroom under which federal law?

    A. Public Law 91-230, Specific Learning Disabilities Act

    B. Public Law 93-112, Rehabilitation Act, Section 504

    C. Public Law 94-142, Education for All Handicapped Children Act

    D. Public Law 101-476, Individuals with Disabilities Education Act

Answer: B

Rationale (18): By law, students with ADD (or ADHD, hyperactivity included), MUST receive special **accommodations** in the regular classroom when documented evidence shows such a need (e.g., a letter from the physician treating the youngster). Attention Deficit Disorder is not listed as a separate special education category in the special education laws (e.g., Public Laws 91-230, 94-142, or 101-476). Public Law 93-112 mandates that students with ADD (or ADHD) receive **reasonable accommodations** needed in order to help them learn.

ELEMENTARY SAMPLE QUESTIONS

19. Which is UNTRUE about youngsters with social maladjustments?

A. They have values and/or behaviors that are in conflict with the school, home, or community.

B. They are eligible for and served under the special education exceptionality category of Emotional/Behavioral Disorders.

C. They maintain a consistent pattern of aberrant and antisocial behavior.

D. They show few, if any, sighs of guilt, remorse, or concern for the feelings of others.

Answer: B

Rationale (19): Students with social maladjustments are eligible to receive services for Emotional/Behavioral Disorders only if they have documented eligibility for this special education exceptionality category as well. Youngsters with **social maladjustments** have characteristics that include: values and/or behaviors in conflict with the school, home, or community; a consistent pattern of aberrant and antisocial behavior; and a lack of guilt, remorse, or concern for the feelings of others.

20. _____ is an organic reason for mild learning and behavioral disabilities.

A. Inadequate education

B. Toxins

C. Biochemical factors

D. Maturational lag

Answer: C

21. An environmental reason for mild learning and behavioral disabilities is

   A. Poverty

   B. Genetics

   C. Biochemical factors

   D. Maturational lag

Answer: A

Rationales (20 & 21): Causes for mild disabilities can primarily be subdivided into two major categories: organic (biological) and environmental. Included under **environmental** reasons for mild learning and behavior disabilities are factors relating to poverty, nutrition, toxins, language differences, sensory deprivation, emotional problems, and inadequate education. Under the **organic** category, factors relating to pre-, peri-, and postnatal conditions, genetics, biochemical, and maturational lag are noted. These contributors originate within the body (i.e., they are endogenous). Overlap between the environmental and organic categories sometimes occurs. For example, even though some environmental factors (e.g., toxins) cause organic dysfunction, the point of origin is outside the body (i.e., exogenous).

Teaching Methods and Strategies

1. **A student's functional capabilities and entry level skills are best measured by**

    A. Norm-referenced tests

    B. Criterion-referenced tests

    C. Standardized intelligence tests

    D. Teacher-made unit quizzes

Answer: B

Rationale (1): Results from **criterion-referenced** tests give measures of progress made by students in learning specific skills in terms of level of mastery. The content of criterion-referenced tests is based on a specified set of objectives. This type of test enables the teacher to determine the specific point at which to begin instruction, and to plan the instructional content at the student's level of functioning that follows in sequence in the curriculum.

2. **A prerequisite skill is essentially**

    A. The smallest component of any skill

    B. A tool for accomplishing task analysis

    C. A skill that must be demonstrated before instruction on a specific task can begin.

    D. The lowest order skill in a hierarchy of skills needed to perform a specific task.

Answer: C

Rationale (2): Learning generally occurs in a step-by-step, sequential manner. A **prerequisite skill** is a skill that a student must master in order to develop subsequent skills.

3. **All of the following are suggestions for when to alter the presentation of tasks to match the students' rate of learning EXCEPT**

 A. Find a teaching approach that works and do not vary from it.

 B. Teach in several shorter segments of time rather than a single lengthy session.

 C. Watch for nonverbal cues that indicate students are becoming confused, bored, or restless.

 D. Avoid giving students an inappropriate amount of written work.

Answer: A

Rationale (3): The teacher must vary the style as well as the content of instructional lessons. The successful teacher applies a **variety of approaches** in teaching content, just as she varies content material to maintain student interest.

4. **Which will contribute least to the quality of Lisa's long-term memory of multiplication facts? Lisa**

 A. Was attentive and watched as her teacher demonstrated multiplication groups with hands-on manipulatives and on the chalkboard.

 B. Is interested in learning multiplication facts

 C. Participates in math games and drills which promote over learning

 D. Was given a worksheet of multiples of sixes to memorize for homework

Answer: D

Rationale (4): **Long-term memory** requires the storage of information for an extended period of time before efforts are made to retrieve this information. Long-term memory is enhanced when a student demonstrates a meaningful understanding of the information through first hand experiences, when the student is interested in learning the information, and when the student is given the opportunity to participate in activities which promote overlearning.

5. **Which factors are reported to have an effect upon long-term memory?**

   A. Cognitive functions

   B. Effective strategies

   C. Situational variables

   D. All of the above

Rationale (5): Cognitive thinking skills, the use of effective learning strategies, and situational variables have all been reported to have an effect upon long-term memory.

6. **Brian's teacher has observed that he has difficulty making letters legible, and cannot stay on the line or space them adequately. Which instructional strategy might be used by his teacher that keeps distributive practice time and motivation in mind in order to assist him with improving his handwriting skills?**

   A. Require Brian to write one letter each day for an hour.

   B. Provide Brian with a variety of ways to work on forming letters during brief practice sessions with breaks.

   C. Have Brian copy a few selected letters for a full writing period.

   D. Have Brian write one letter for ten minutes and then allow free activity time
   for the remainder of the class period.

Answer: B

Rationale (6): There are two diverse methods for programming practice and study time. **Massed practice** extends over a longer block of time; whereas, **distributive** practice divides time into several shorter intervals, with rest between the time periods. **Distributive practice** time for handwriting skills involving fine motor coordination would best be done during shorter time intervals to sustain focus, energy, and motivation.

7. **According to Cawley, when teachers call out spelling words during a Friday quiz and have the students write the words after they are spoken, the interactive instructional presentations and response requirements used are those of**

   A. Construct-write

   B. State-write

   C. Write-present

   D. State-construct

Answer: B

Rationale (7): The **interactive unit instructional model** outlined by Cawley (1986) allows for sixteen different combinations of teacher input and student output. In this example, the teacher "states" and the students "write."

8. **Which is LEAST likely to enable a student to function independently in a learning environment such as the classroom?**

   A. The learner must understand the nature of the assignment.

   B. The student must be able to do the assigned task.

   C. The teacher must communicate performance criteria to the learner.

   D. The learner must be able to find someone to explain the content to him or her.

Answer: D

Rationale (8): In order for self-sufficiency to occur in the academic setting, the teacher must set the environment and make assurances that the student can function independently. Several factors must be addressed, before independent functioning can be expected. The student must "understand" what is required and be "able" to do the work. Initially, the teacher must provide encouragement and offer guidance, assistance, and prompting, when needed. Finally, the task expectations held by the teacher must be conveyed to the student (i.e., how they should be done and criteria for successful completion). (Ramsey, 1995)

9. **In the following example, which statement would best indicate that the teacher is responding to a student's feelings and not just his verbal message? Marty, when given back his science test, rushes up to Mr. Page's desk, points to his test paper, and exclaims somewhat angrily, "This is unfair! You didn't say that this would be on the test."**

   A. "Go back and sit down!"

   B. "I specifically said that the entire chapter would be on the test."

   C. "You're saying that you're upset because you didn't do well on the test."

   D. "If had listened carefully during the review you would have known what to study."

Answer: C

Rationale (9): To facilitate communication, the teacher must become an active listener. At times, it is essential that the teacher listen to what the student is really saying, make a response to the student which the teacher thinks reflects the student's feeling about the matter. By responding to the child's feelings, the teacher lets the person know his or her understanding of the matter. The student is encouraged to communicate further.

10. **Immediate rather than delayed feedback is appropriately used when a student is**

   A. Exhibiting behaviors that are disturbing to others.

   B. Experiencing difficulty with an assigned task.

   C. Attempting to correct his mistakes.

   D. Making errors practicing a newly introduced skill.

Answer: D

Rationale (10): The timing of teacher feedback to students is important. There are appropriate uses for both **immediate** and **delayed feedback** in the classroom in learning situations. When learning new skills, or practicing tasks still to be mastered, **immediate** and specific feedback regarding performance is necessary. Giving **delayed** feedback is beneficial when students are trying to correct their own mistakes, discover their own answers, and review previously learned skills.

ELEMENTARY SAMPLE QUESTIONS   168

11. **The preventive discipline technique of proximity control is shown when the teacher**
    A. Moves closer to the student who is showing signs of difficulty.
    B. Uses signals to communicate disapproval to the student.
    C. Shows interest in the student at crucial times.
    D. Expresses humor to lessen tension.

Answer: A

Rationale (11): Teachers use preventive discipline techniques to nullify potential or budding discipline problems. Good classroom management requires the ability to select appropriate intervention strategies from an array of alternatives. **Proximity control** is used when teachers move close to a student or small group of students, and stand behind or beside the main perpetrator, make direct eye contract, or gently place a hand on a student's shoulder to stop a disturbing behavior.

12. **The teacher might determine which of the following activities to be most appropriate in developing a child's decision-making abilities?**

    A. Ask the child to participate in show-and-tell activities.

    B. Place the child in charge of a small, manageable part of his environment to ensure success.

    C. Create a situation in which a choice has to be made and present plausible options from which the child must select one and be able to defend it.

    D. Develop role-playing situations in which the child expresses his feelings about being teased.

Answer: C

Rationale (12): Children require conscious instruction in personal and social development dimensions. Some children lack the self-confidence to make decisions. Teachers can help these youngsters strengthen their decisions-making capabilities by creating situations (e.g., stories, role play, hypothetical situations) in which children must consider alternatives and make decisions about them.

13. Which is true about self-concept?

A. Self-concept is the collective attitudes or feelings which a child has about himself or herself.

B. Self-concept is formed in part from attitudes held by others.

C. A person's weaknesses and how he or she perceives them may affect the development of personal self-concept.

D. All of the above are true.

Answer: D

Rationale (13): **Self-concept** can be defined as the collective attitudes or feelings which one holds about oneself. These attitudes and feeling are formed in part by the attitudes and reactions of others and the way in which the youngsters have been treated by them. Continuing efforts should be made to better each child's own perception of him or herself.

14. Theorists like L. A. Kohlberg have purported that a person's morality is achieved in developmental stages. At which level do children view right and wrong by consequences of their actions?

A. Preconventional

B. Conventional

C. Postconventional

Answer: A

Rationale (14): A taxonomy for moral development includes three main developmental stages. At the **preconventional level**, right and wrong are understood by children as "good or bad" consequences. Social approval, psychological payoff, and personal gain are associated with right and wrong at the **conventional level** which generally occurs at adolescence. At the **postconventional level**, awareness of the rights of others are acknowledged, and issues are viewed as right or wrong based upon substantive judgments about their content. Some adults never reach this level unfortunately.

15. In the behavioral objective, "Given a worksheet with multiplication facts on it, Sam will write correct answers to 18 of the 20," the phrase. . . "will write correct answers" . . . is the

   A. Condition

   B. Behavior

   C. Criterion

Answer: B

Rationale (15): A behavioral objective contains three major components: condition, behavior, and criterion. The **condition** states under what condition the behavior will occur. The **behavior** is given as a verb or verb phrase that can be defined, observed and measured. The **criterion** tells how much of the behavior is to be demonstrated in order for the objective to be met.

16. Jack's teacher has discovered that Jack needs continuous feedback in order to experience small, incremental achievements. What type of instructional material would best meet this need?

   A. Programmed materials

   B. Audiotapes

   C. Materials with no writing required

   D. Worksheets

Answer: A

Rationale (16): **Programmed materials** offer step-by-step, sequential instruction in small increments, with immediate feedback that lets the learner know the correctness or incorrectness of each response. These materials are useful in developing learner independence and in teaching students to self-manage their learning experiences.

17. **Mr. Hardy was delighted to find an excellent math kit, published by a well- known company, on sale at her local school supply house. She had wanted to purchase this kit for a long time, but had been unable to fit it into her budget. Now, however, the entire kit, including flashcards, charts, booklets, and thirty individual student workbooks, was priced at only 40 percent of the regular price. Upon inquiry, Mr. Hardy learned that the kit was on sale because it was no longer being produced by the publisher. For what reason did Mr. Hardy later regret purchasing the kit?**

A. The cost was under the amount that his budget allowed him to spend for school supplies.

B. Consumable worksheets were out of print and unable to be reordered.

C. The materials in the kit covered a wide range of student skills.

D. The materials were easily stored.

Answer: B

18. **A money bingo game was designed by Mr. Phillips for use with his middle grade students. Cards were constructed with different combinations of coins pasted on each of the nine spaces. Mr. Phillips called out various amounts of change (e.g., 45 cents) and students were instructed to cover the coin combinations on their cards which equaled the amount of change (e.g., four dimes and one nickel, one quarter and two dimes, and so on). The student who had the first bingo was required to add the coins in each of the spaces covered and tell their amounts before being declared the winner. Eight of Mr. Phillips seventh graders played the game in the learning center the first day the game was constructed. Which of the following attributes are present in this game used in this manner?**

   A. Players can use the activity independently to reinforce skills.

   B. A teacher must supervise players.

   C. The game is of lengthy duration.

   D. Players will find game too easy.

Answer: A

Rationales (17 and 18): The selection, development, and adaptation of instructional materials is a significant responsibility all teachers have in order to teach students. Materials must be flexible to cover diverse functioning levels and repetitive practice needs. Teachers must consider the characteristics of effective teaching materials, such as quality, durability, utility, and cost effectiveness. Physical, sensory, social, and intellectual strengths and limitations of students must include materials with which students can be self-directed and utilized independently.

Classroom Management

1. **Mickey does a lot of attention-seeking behaviors in Mrs. Green's fourth grade class. If he isn't making "cute" remarks, he is throwing paper, tapping on his desk with his fingers, or most anything to get his classmates to laugh at him. the most effective nonverbal intervention that could be used by Mrs. Green would probably be for her and the other students to remove the reinforcement of responding to Mickey by applying**

   A. Planned ignoring

   B. Signal interference

   C. Proximity control

   D. Removal of seductive objects

Answer: A

Rationale (1): In applying **planned ignoring**, the teacher purposefully ignores the child's behavior, thus removing a viable reinforcer, that of teacher attention. This technique works with attention seeking and minor disruptive behaviors, but should not be used if the behavior is of a severe, harmful, or self-injurious nature.

2. **Teachers who alert students to changes in activities by giving them time to make adjustments to these changes are using the verbal intervention called**

   A. Humor

   B. Restructuring

   C. Alerting

   D. Hypodermic affection

Answer: C

Rationale (2): Making abrupt changes from one activity to another can bring on behavior problems. **Alerting** helps students to make smooth transitions by giving them time to make emotional adjustments to change.

3. **Sometimes students get frustrated, discouraged, and anxious in school. Saying a kind word, giving a smile, or   just showing interest in a child gives the encouragement that is needed. This often highly effective verbal intervention is referred to as**

    A. Humor

    B. Restructuring

    C. Alerting

    D. Hypodermic affection

Answer: D

Rationale (3): The technique **hypodermic affection** gives a boost to students who are feeling frustrated, discouraged, or anxious in school. Saying a kind word, giving a smile, or just showing interest in a child gives the encouragement that is needed. **Hypodermic affection** lets students know they are valued.

4. **Which is an example of engaged learning time?**

    A. Mr. Williams schedules 30 minutes a day for sustained silent reading.

    B. Jane has 5 minutes to shower and dress after her Physical Education class.

    C. Jerry wrote answers to five social studies questions during a continuous 45 minute work time at his desk.

    D. Mrs. Brown instructs students to do boardwork while she conduct three reading groups for an hour each morning.

Answer: C

Rationale (4): **Engaged learning time** refers to the amount of time that a student is actually working on task. **Allocated time** is the amount of time scheduled for a specific subject.

5. _____ is a method of structuring small groups of students so that all the individuals achieve a learning goal through mutual planning and decision making.

   A. Peer tutoring

   B. Behavior modification

   C. Direct instruction

   D. Cooperative learning

Answer: D

Rationale (5): **Cooperative learning** is a method of structuring small groups of students so that everyone achieves his or her learning goal through mutual planning and decision making.

6. Behaviorists believe that all behavior, appropriate or inappropriate, is

   A. Predictable

   B. Learned

   C. Observed

   D. Conditioned

Answer: B

Rationale (6): Proponents of behavior modification contend that ALL behavior is **learned**.

7. A positive reinforcer is generally effective if it is given only upon the occurrence of the target behavior and

A. Given immediately after the desired behavior.

B. Given in worthwhile amounts (appropriate in size).

C. Given when the student has been deprived of it.

D. All of the above.

Answer: D

Rationale (7): Four basic principles for applying effective reinforcement state that
the reinforcer must be
1) administered **immediately**
2) **contingent** upon the specified behavior
3) be **worthwhile**, that is, of appropriate size to the behavior emitted
4) administered following **deprivation** of that behavior

Special Education Law

1. **A ruling pertaining to the use of evaluation procedures which was immersed into the federal legislation of Public Law 94-142 and Public Law 101-476 resulted from which court case?**

   A. Diana v. the State Board of Education (1970)

   B. Wyatt v. Stickney (1971)

   C. Larry P. v. Riles (1979)

   D. PASE v. Hannon (1980)

Answer: A

Rationale (1): Diana v. the State of Board of Education (1970) resulted in the decision that all children must be tested in their native language. Wyatt v. Stickney (1971) established the right to adequate treatment (education) for institutionalized persons with mental retardation. Larry P. v. Riles (1979) ordered the re-evaluation of Black students enrolled in classes for mild mental retardation (then called educable mentally retarded or EMR, and enjoined the California State Department of Education from the use of intelligence tests in subsequent placement decisions. Parents in Action on Special Education (PASE) v. Hannon ruled that IQ tests are not necessarily biased against ethnic and racial subcultures.

2. **Which are recognized as being the most important political forces whose efforts resulted in obtaining the regulations and mandates contained within Public Law 94-142 and Public Law 101-476?**

   A. Actions taken by parent and professional support groups

   B. Public laws put into effect

   C. Rulings from court cases

   D. All of these were important influences

Answer: D

Rationale (2): Three important political forces were instrumental in obtaining the forerunner legislation and litigation which is now subsumed within Public Law 94-142 (and now, Public Law 101-576). These important forces include: 1) parent and professional support groups, 2) reform legislation, and 3) adversary litigation.

3. Which is the status of Public Law 94-142 at the present time?

A. Medical lifesaving forces have cured children with disabilities.

B. Public Law 94-142 suffered service and financial cutbacks during the 1980s and 1990s.

C. Public Law 94-142 has been re-authorized as Public Law 101-476, with changes primarily in terminology, procedural planning for transition, and the formation of two new categories.

D. Major expansion of services to infants, preschoolers, and secondary youth occurred in the 1990 Amendment.

Answer: C

Rationale (3): At the present time, Public Law 94-142 (the Education for ALL Handicapped Children Act), has been re-authorized as Public Law 101-476 (the Individuals with Disabilities Education Act), with changes primarily in terminology, procedural planning for transition, and the formation of two new exceptionality categories: Autism and Traumatic Brain Injury.

4. **Which of the following examples would be considered of highest priority when determining the need for the delivery of appropriate special education and related services?**

   A. Eight-year-old boy who is repeating first grade for the second time and exhibits problems with toileting, gross motor functions, and remembering number or letter symbols. His regular classroom teacher claims the referral forms are too time consuming and refuses to fill them out. She refuses to make accommodations because she believes every child should be treated alike.

   B. Six-year-old girl who has been diagnosed as autistic and placed in a special education class within the local school. Her mother wants her to attend a residential school next year, even though the girl is showing progress.

   C. Ten-year-old girl with profound mental retardation who is receiving educational services in a state institution.

   D. Twelve-year-old boy with mild disabilities who was placed in a behavior disorders resource program, but displays obvious perceptual deficits (e.g., reversals of letters and symbols, inability to discriminate sounds). He was originally thought to have a learning disability, but did not meet state criteria for this exceptionality category based on results of standard scores. He has always had problems with attending to a task, and is now beginning to get into trouble during seatwork time. His teacher feels that he will eventually become a real behavior problem. He receives social skills training in the resource room one period a day.

Answer: A

Rationale (4): **Priorities** identified in the legislation for the delivery of services and appropriation of federal funds are: (1) children with disabilities not receiving any education, and (2) children with the most severe disabilities receiving inappropriate education. The first example given was about a youngster with disabling characteristics whose teacher had refused to make accommodations for or even refer for special education.

5. Safeguards against bias and discrimination in the assessment of children include

A. The testing of a child in standard English.

B. The requirement for the use of one standardized test.

C. The use of evaluation materials in the child's native language or other mode of communication.

D. All testing performed by a certified, licensed psychologist.

Answer: C

Rationale (5): Evaluation of students for special education must be **nondiscriminary**. Tests must be administered in the child's native language or other mode of communication. They must be validated for the specific purpose for which they are intended. Testing instruments must be tailored to assess specific areas of educational need and areas related to the suspected disability. Evaluation must be made by a multidisciplinary team. No single test (procedure) may be used as the sole criterion for determining placement or an appropriate educational program.

6. The Individuals with Disabilities Education Act (IDEA) was signed into law as an Amendment to the Education of ALL Handicapped children Act (EHA) in

A. 1975

B. 1980

C. 1990

D. 1995

Answer: C

Rationale (6): The EHA Amendments of 1990 (Public Law 101-476) were signed into law by President Bush on October 30, 1990. This action renamed the EHA as the Individuals with Disabilities Education Act (IDEA).

7. A specific change in the language in IDEA is which of the following?

A. The term "disorder" changed to "disability"

B. The term "children" changed to "children and youth"

C. The term "handicaps" changed to "impairments"

D. The term "handicapped" changed to "with disabilities"

Answer: D

Rationale (7): Changes in **terminology** included the following: "children" became "individuals," meaning that some of the students with special needs are adolescents and young adults--not just children. "Handicapped" was changed to "with disabilities." This signified the difference between limitations imposed by society (handicap) and an inability to do certain things (disability). The phrase "with disabilities" demostrates that the disabled condition is only one characteristic of the individual; it is not his or her whole persona.

8. The family plays a vital role in our society by

A. Assuming a protective and nurturing function.

B. Acting as the primary unit for social control.

C. Playing a major role in the transmission of cultural values and mores.

D. All of the above.

Answer: D

Rationale (8): The correct answer is "d." The family plays a vital role in our society by: (a) assuming a protective and nurturing function, (b) acting as the primary unit for social control, and (c) playing a major role in the transmission of cultural values and mores.

9. **George is a three-year-old boy who has recently overcome a bout with meningitis. The pediatrician who treated George during his illness had to inform George's parents about brain dysfunction which he medically diagnosed. The first reaction in a series of parent reactions which the doctor should anticipate when informing George's parents about his medical findings would be that of**

   A. Denial
   B. Shock
   C. Disbelief
   D. Helplessness

Answer: B

Rationale (9): The discovery of a child's disabling condition has a strong impact on the family. Though reactions are unique to persons, the first emotion generally felt by a parent of a child with a disability is **shock**, followed by disbelief, guilt, rejection, shame, denial, and helplessness. The feeling of acceptance is generally the last to come about, and even with acceptance, many parents report periods of anxiety and fearfulness about their personal ability to care for their exceptional child.

10. **The terms "support," "assistance," and "appraisal" are likely to be used**

   A. When making formal referrals of students for special education.

   B. For school-based teams of educators that are formed to solve learning and behavior problems for special students in the regular classroom.

   C. By school psychologists when evaluating students for special education.

   D. By school boards when facing an audit or monitoring session.

Answer: B

Rationale (10): Federal legislation requires that prior to referral for special education, sincere efforts be made to help students found to be at-risk academically or socially. In most states, school-based teams of educators are formed to solve learning and behavior problems in the regular classroom. These informal problem-solving teams have an assortment of names that include concepts of **support** (school support teams, student support teams), **assistance** (teacher assistance teams, school assistance teams), and **appraisal** (school appraisal teams) (Pugach & Johnson, 1989). Regardless of the name, the purpose for the teams is similar.

11. Summaries of a student's educational strengths and weaknesses are recorded on the IEP (individualized education plan) as

A. Short-team objectives

B. Annual goals

C. Current levels of performance

D. Related services

Answer: C

Rationale (11): Educational strengths and weaknesses are recorded on students' IEPs as current levels of performance.

12. Which is TRUE about IDEA? To be eligible, a student must

A. Have a medical disability

B. Have a disability that fits into one of the categories listed in the law

C. Attend a private school

D. Be a slow learner

Answer: B

Rationale (12): To be eligible for special education, it is stated in IDEA that a student must have a disability that fits into one of the categories listed in this law.

13. Which is UNTRUE about the Americans with Disabilities Act (ADA)?

    A. Re-authorized discretionary programs of EHA.

    B. Signed into law the same year as IDEA by President Bush.

    C. Gives protections to all people on the basis of race, sex, national origin, and religion.

    D. Guarantees equal opportunities to persons with disabilities in employment, public accommodations, transportation, government services, and telecommunications.

Answer: A

Rationale (13): The Americans with Disabilities Act (ADA) was signed into law in 1990 by President Bush (as was IDEA). The ADA gives protections to all people on the basis of race, sex, national origin, and religion. It guarantees equal opportunities to persons with disabilities in employment, public accommodations, transportation, government services, and telecommunications. ADA did not reauthorize discretionary programs of EHA.

14. What does NOT determine whether a person is entitled to protection under Public Law 93-112, Section 504, the Rehabilitation Act?

    A. The individual must meet the definition of a person with a disability.

    B. The person must be able to meet the requirements of a particular program in spite of his or her disability.

    C. The person must be eligible for a special education categorical service under IDEA.

    D. The school, business, or other facility must be a recipient of federal funding assistance.

Answer: C

Rationale (14): In order to be entitled to protection under Public Law 93-112, Section 504, the Rehabilitation Act, there are several requirements. The person must meet the definition of a person with a disability, but it is not necessary for the person to be eligible for a special education category under IDEA. The person must be able to meet the requirements of a particular program in spite of his or her disability. The school, business, or other facility must be a recipient of federal funding assistance.

15. Janice is a third grader. Mrs. Green, her teacher, noted that Janice was having difficulty with math and reading assignments. The results from recent diagnostic tests showed a strong sight vocabulary, strength in computational skills, but a weakness in comprehending what she had read. This weakness was apparent in mathematical word problems as well. The multidisciplinary team recommended placement in a special education resource room for learning disabilities two periods each school day. For the remainder of the school day, her placement will be

A. In the regular classroom

B. At a special school

C. In a self-contained classroom

D. In a resource room for students with mental retardation

Answer: A

Rationale (15): Most students like Janice, with **mild** disabilities, and in particular those served in resource rooms for one to several periods a day, remain in the regular classroom for the major portion of the school day. Students receiving special services through consultation or inclusion function for the entire day in the regular classroom.

16. **Jim shows behavior problems like lack of attention, out-of-seat behavior, and talking out. His teacher has kept data on these behaviors and has found that Jim is showing much better self-control since he has been self-managing himself through a behavior modification program. The most appropriate placement recommendation for Jim at this time is probably**

    A. Any available part-time special education program

    B. The regular classroom solely

    C. A behavior disorders resource room for one period a day

    D. A specific learning disabilities resource room for one period a day

Answer: B

Rationale (16): Children like Jim, whose learning and social-interpersonal problems tend to be of a mild and easily correctable nature, can be taught successfully in the **regular** classroom by a regular classroom teacher. Thus far, the self-management intervention is working with Jim and he should remain in the regular classroom.

17. **Which of the following would be classified as direct rather than indirect services that specially trained special education teachers would provide for regular education teachers?**

    A. Answer questions about a particular child's academic or social-interpersonal needs

    B. Develop math worksheets tailored to meet a student's needs

    C. Assist with selecting special materials for a student

    D. Teach a math unit on measurement

Answer: D

Rationale (17): There are two types of services that special education teachers deliver in the schools, and these are **direct** and **indirect** services. Through **direct** services, the special education teacher comes into the regular classroom and co-teaches with the general education teacher. In this capacity, the special education teacher works with individuals, small groups, and large groups of students who are experiencing similar educational difficulties.

ELEMENTARY SAMPLE QUESTIONS

18. **Which is a "less than ideal" example of collaboration in successful inclusion?**

    A. Special education teachers are a part of the instructional team in a regular classroom.

    B. Special education teachers assist regular education teachers in the classroom.

    C. Teaming approaches are used for problem-solving and program implementation.

    D. Regular teachers, special education teachers, and other specialists or support teachers co-teach.

Answer: B

Rationale (18): Successful **collaboration** includes regular teachers, special education teachers, and other specialists working together as equals. This is done by co-teaching, team teaching, and working together on teacher assistance teams.

19. **In successful inclusion**

    A. A variety of instructional arrangements is available

    B. School personnel shift the responsibility for learning outcomes to the students

    C. The physical facilities are used as they are

    D. Regular classroom teachers have sole responsibility for evaluating student progress

Answer: A

Rationale (19): In successful **inclusion** a variety of instructional arrangements is available. Responsibility for learning outcomes are shared between teachers and students. Curriculum-based measurement is used to systematically assess students' learning progress. Facilities are adaptable to student needs.

20. Which of the following is "uncharacteristic" of a resource room program?

   A. It has a specially trained teacher.

   B. The students are in attendance there all day.

   C. The students spend the majority of the school day in the regular classroom.

   D. It is intended to supplement regular school progress.

Answer: B

Rationale (20): **Resource room** programs are characterized as regularly scheduled instructional settings to which students go during the day for brief periods of special instruction. This is intended to supplement regular school progress for specific academic and social skills areas. Teachers are specially trained and students spend the majority of the school day in the regular classroom.

21. Which of the following is "characteristic" of students receiving special services in a resource room?

   A. Causes of disabling conditions are easily identifiable.

   B. Physical appearance of students are easily identifiable.

   C. Students share a variety of behaviors that cut across characteristics associated with traditional categories.

   D. Students are able to meet academic and behavioral standards in regular classroom settings.

Answer: C

Rationale (21): Students receiving resource room services share a variety of behaviors that cut across characteristics associated with traditional special education categories (e.g., Mental Retardation, Specific Learning Disabilities, Emotional/Behavioral Disorders). Furthermore, these students appear the same as regular classroom students, have etiologies or causes that are mostly unknown, and receive serves because they are unable to meet academic and behavioral standards in all regular classroom settings.

22. In general, students determined eligible for resource room placement

   A. Are identifiable in appearance from their grade-level peers.

   B. Are able to succeed academically without special services.

   C. Are evaluated as moderately disabled.

   D. Are unidentifiable once they enter the labor force.

Answer: D

Rationale (22): Most students with mild disabilities who received special education in resource room are not perceivably different when they enter the world of work.

23. Which is not a major responsibility of a teacher of a self contained special education classroom?

   A. Teaches most subjects

   B. Is responsible for planning most student instruction

   C. Works with students in several special education categories

   D. Implements most of the instruction during the day

Answer: C

Rationale (23): Students generally are assigned by exceptionality category to self-contained, special education classrooms. A specially trained teacher is responsible for planning student instruction, implementing the instruction during the school day, and teaching most subject areas.

24. Which is least indicative of a developmental delay?

    A. Language and speech production

    B. Gross motor skills

    C. Self-help skills

    D. Arithmetic computation skills

Answer: D

Rationale (24): Preschool youngsters with moderate disabilities generally demonstrate **developmental delays** in the areas of language and communication, gross motor skills, social-interpersonal skills, and rudimentary self-help and adaptive skills (e.g., walking, dressing, toileting).

25. Inappropriate behaviors displayed by children at the moderate level of severity who are placed in a self-contained education class are generally characterized as

    A. Significant in degree and intensity

    B. Relatively the same in number as those exhibited by the general population

    C. Acceptable to the child and his peers

    D. In line with the child's chronological age

Answer: A

Rationale (25): Inappropriate behaviors displayed by children at the **moderate** level of severity are characterized as exhibiting behaviors that are significantly excessive, disruptive, and inappropriate. The number, as well as the degree and intensity of the behaviors, is comparatively high. The problem behaviors often interfere with the student's expected performance (e.g., intellectual, social-interpersonal, adaptive) relative to chronological age.

26. Placement at a special school is considered to be a "less restrictive environment" than which?

    A. Regular classroom

    B. Inclusive setting

    C. Self-contained special education classroom

    D. Homebound

Answer: D

Rationale (26): Placement at a special school is considered to be a **less restrictive environment** than that of homebound. Evelyn Deno's Cascade System of Special Education Services extend form least to most restrictive, respectively: regular classroom, regular classroom with supportive services (i.e., consultation, inclusion), regular classroom with part-time special class (i.e., itinerant services, resource room), full-time special class (i.e., self-contained), special stations (i.e., special schools), homebound, and residential (hospital, institution).

27. Which is most descriptive of vocational training in special education?

    A. Trains students with intellectual disabilities solely.

    B. Segregates students with and without disabilities in vocational training programs.

    C. Only includes students capable of moderate supervision.

    D. Instruction focuses upon self-help skills, social-interpersonal skills, motor skills, rudimentary academic skills, basic occupational skills, and lifetime leisure and recreational skills.

Answer: D

Rationale (27): Formerly, **vocational training** in special education focused upon the exceptional area of intellectual disabilities. Special guidance and training services have more recently been directed toward students in other exceptionality areas like learning disabilities, emotional/behavioral disorders, and physical impairments. Training provisions include special programs for school-aged children and secondary-level adolescents. Instruction focuses upon self-help skills, social-interpersonal skills, motor skills, rudimentary academic skills, basic occupational skills, and lifetime leisure and recreational skills.

28. **In career education, specific training and preparation required for the world of work occurs during the phase of**

A. Career awareness

B. Career exploration

C. Career preparation

D. Daily living and personal-social interaction

Answer: C

Rationale (28): **Career education** attempts to prepare individuals for all facets of life. Curricular aspects of career education include the phases of : (a) career awareness (diversity of available jobs); (b) career exploration (skills needed for occupational groups); and (c) career preparation (specific training and preparation required for the world of work). Career education emphasizes the importance of acquiring skills in the areas of daily living, personal-social interaction, and occupational training and preparation.

Reference List

Billstein, R., Libeskind, S., & Lott, J. W. (1990). A problem solving approach to mathematics for elementary school teachers (4th. ed.). Redwood City, CA: The Benjamin/Cummings Publishing Company, Inc.

Brewer, J. A. (1995). Introduction to early childhood education. (2nd ed.). Allyn & Bacon.

Carnine, D., Silbert, J., & Kameenui, E. J. (1990). Direct instruction reading (2nd ed.). Columbus, OH: Merrill Publishing Company.

Consultants et. al. (1988). Invitation to mathematics. Glenview, IL: Scott Foresman and Company.

DeVries, H. A. (1986). Physiology of exercise for physical education and athletics (4th ed.). Dubuque IA: Wm. C. Brown Publishers.

Eichstaedt, C. B., & Kalakian, L. H. (1993). Developmental/adapted physical education (3rd ed.). New York, NY: Macmillan Publishing Company.

Ellis, A. K. (1991). Teaching and learning elementary social studies (4th ed.). Boston, MA: Allyn and Bacon.

Gega, P. C. (1995). Science in elementary education (7th ed.). New York, NY: Macmillan Publishing Company.

Gleason, J. B. (1993). The development of language (3rd ed.). New York, NY: Macmillan Publishing Company.

Heinich, R., Molenda, M., & Russell, J. D. (1993). Instructional media and the new technologies of instruction (4th ed.). New York, NY: Macmillan Publishing Company.

Henley, M., Ramsey, R. S., & Algozzine, R. (1996). Characteristics of and strategies for teaching students with mild disabilities (2nd ed.). Boston, MA: Allyn and Bacon.

Lefrancois, G. R. (1996). The lifespan (5th ed.). Belmont, CA: Wadsworth Publishing Company.

Norton, D. E. (1993). The effective teaching of language arts (4th ed.). New York, NY: Macmillan Publishing Company.

Nowlan R. A., & Lowe, C. (1977). Lessons in essential mathematics book 1: Arithmetic. New York, NY: Harper & Row, Publishers.

Pangrazi, R. P. & Dauer, V. P. (1995). <u>Dynamic physical education for elementary school children</u> (11th ed.). Boston, MA: Allyn and Bacon.

Ramsey, R. S. (1995). <u>Preparatory guide for special education teacher competency tests- revised.</u> (formerly published by Allyn and Bacon, Boston, MA.)

Rothstein, A. (1995). <u>Special education law.</u> New York, NY: West Publishing Company.

Silbert, J., Carnine, D., & Stein, M. (1990). <u>Direct instruction mathematics</u> (2nd ed.). Columbus, OH: Merrill Publishing Co.

"Mrs. Hammond, I'd know you anywhere from little Billy's portrait of you."

"Are we there yet?"

"Gosh, now we've seen everything!"